To Jerry,
I hope you go
up to visit West Point.
Best wishes,
Eric O—

Be Thou at Peace

The Cemetery at West Point, NY
A Resting Place for Warriors

To Jerre
A delight to know your
wonderful daughters
Ed Blute
Oct 2013

Be Thou at Peace

The Cemetery at West Point, NY
A Resting Place for Warriors

by

Edward A. Blomstedt

Expanding upon the original title
Home at Rest
by
Thomas E. O'Neil

Barton Cove
Publishing
Gill, Massachusetts

A Resting Place for Warriors....

"You are the leaven which binds together the entire fabric of our national system of defense. From your ranks come the great captains who hold the Nation's destiny in their hands the moment the war tocsin sounds....

This does not mean that you are warmongers. On the contrary, the soldier above all other people prays for peace, for he must suffer and bear the deepest wounds and scars of war. But always in our ears ring the ominous words of Plato, that wisest of all philosophers: "Only the dead have seen the end of war."

Douglas MacArthur in his farewell address to the
Corps of Cadets, 1962

"Make no mistake. You will serve in perilous times. The history of the United States will be written with the blood of your classmates. That has been true since 1802. Your class will not be an exception."

General John W. Vessey, Army Chief of Staff, addressing the
Class of 1998 and their families at the Graduation Dinner

Barton Cove Publishing
78 French King Highway
Gill, MA 01354
413.863.2435
bartoncovepublishing@gmail.com

Be Thou at Peace website: www.blackgraygold.com

Cadet photographs courtesy of US Military Academy

Veterans Day 1997 by Jamie Malanowski. West Point, N.Y.
Copyright ©TIME INC. Reprinted by permission. Time is a registered trademark of Time Inc. All rights reserved.

At West Point, A Quiet Place to Honor Warriors, by Rick Hampson, December 27, 2011, from USA TODAY, a division of Gannett Co., Inc. Reprinted with permission.

ISBN 978-0-9819555-0-6

Printed in the United States of America
First printing

Dedicated to the

West Point Classes of '98
1898…1998…2098

and especially #54821 in that Long Gray Line

Honoring the Service of

For a photograph or biography
of your
West Pointer

"They are here in ghostly assemblage.
The ranks of the Corps long dead.
And our hearts are standing attention,
while we wait for their passing tread."

from "The Corps"

Table of Contents

FORWARD

By Jamie Malanowski

Too Many Brave Souls

The Military Academy cemetery rewards the wandering ironist

Walk through the graveyard; cemeteries reward the ironist. The collision between what once was and what is no more, the ineffability of a last impression, the follow-up question that can never be answered— it's all right there. In the cemetery at the U.S. Military Academy at West Point, Veterans Day will pass without formal observation: if the weather holds, the 6,827 men, women and children interred there will spend the day under a cerulean sky and pompon trees,

and the living around them will give them the merest thought. Cemeteries reward the ironist.

Start in a bit from the entrance. There is a stone marking the plot of a Colonel Buchwald. It is large but not enormous, and Buchwald probably served his country well. The site would blend unnoticed if his neighbor to the left, lying under a small government-issue marker, wasn't Norman Cota, the general who on D-day rallied the scattered American

invasion force on Omaha Beach and pushed it past the German defenses; Robert Mitchum played him in The Longest Day. A hundred yards away, under a similarly modest headstone, rests Alonzo H. Cushing, who commanded the federal battery at Gettysburg that stood at the very point Pickett aimed his charge. Cushing, twice wounded, stayed at his guns, firing double canister at the converging Confederates until a third shot got him. Right behind him is buried Judson Kilpatrick, a general considered so profligate with the lives of his men that they called him "Kill Cavalry."

At the end of the row, under an obelisk, lies George Armstrong Custer. Or what may be Custer. When Custer was disinterred a year after the Battle of the Little Bighorn, diggers found that animals had scattered the bones. They took their best guess. Cemeteries reward the ironist.

There are heroes here: Paul Bunker, the only Army player to make Walter Camp's All-America team at two different positions, who died in a Japanese POW camp after smuggling his unit's flag past his captors; Ed White, who walked in space and died in Apollo I; Joe Stilwell of China; Lucius Clay of the Berlin airlift; George Goethals of the Panama Canal. The biggest monument, however, a large pyramid, belongs to a general named Egbert Viele. An eminent engineer, he helped design the cemetery, which perhaps explains his prominence. The entrance to the pyramid is

guarded by a pair of sphinxes. These are not the original sphinxes, which Mrs. Viele found too buxom, and which were then sunk in the Hudson River. Cemeteries reward the ironist.

Walk around. Walter Schulze was assigned to fly the news that the Great War was over to units east of the Rhine; on the way home, his plane crashed and he was killed. Art Bonifas, near the end of his tour, took a group out one day in 1976 to prune a poplar in the DMZ; the North Koreans set upon them and killed him.

In Viet Nam, Ron Zinn, twice an Olympic

race walker, went out on patrol ahead of his unit and stepped on a mine. Bob Fuellhart was advising a Viet Namese battalion; while word was being sent up from the rear that his daughter had just been born, word was being sent back that he had been killed. Cemeteries reward the ironist.

"I got interested in this place," says Lieut. Colonel Conrad Crane, a member of West Point's history department, "when I asked the cadets in my class why they were here. Some said free education or to get a job on Wall Street. I wanted to show them what being a West Pointer is all about." He shows them a graveyard full of the young, dating from the first man buried here in 1782.

Walk along the western edge, and you find the dead of World War II, many of whom perished young. Charles Finley of the class of 1943, killed in Normandy in 1944. Henry Benitez of the class of '42, killed at Falaise in '44. Turner Chambliss Jr, '43, killed June 6, 1944. And so on, until you turn a corner and start finding George Tow and Samuel Coursen of the class of '49, killed in action in Korea,

1950. Over behind the Viele monument are the graves from Viet Nam. There is a row in which 10 of 11 graves are occupied by members of the class of '66, and that does not begin to encompass that class's contribution. When that run ends, you have five in a row from the class of '64. One belongs to John Hottell III -- a Rhodes Scholar, twice a recipient of the Silver Star-- who was killed in 1970. The year before, he had written his own obituary and sent it in a sealed envelope to his wife. "I deny that I died for anything -- not my country, not my Army, not my fellow man," he wrote. "I lived for these things, and the manner in which I chose to do it involved the very real chance that 1 would die ... my love for West Point and the Army was great enough ... for me to accept this possibility as part of a price which must be paid for things of great value." Walk through the graveyard; cemeteries humble the ironist.

Veterans Day 1997

The West Point cemetery provides the final resting place for many distinguished Soldiers, including men and women from every major conflict in our nation's history. Listed below are some notable individuals:

1 **GEN Lucius D. Clay (USMA, 1918):** WWII Allied Commander in Europe. Architect of the Berlin Airlift, which is still hailed as an amazing feat of logistics. XVIII-G-079

2 **GEN Alexander "Sandy" Patch (USMA, 1913):** Commanded the invasion forces at Guadalcanal and the Seventh Army in Europe for the invasion of France. I-C-058

3 **GEN William Westmoreland (USMA, 1936):** Commander of US military forces in Vietnam and later 25th Chief of Staff, US Army. XVIII-F-066

4 **GEN Bernard Rogers (USMA, 1943):** A Rhodes scholar, the 28th Chief of Staff, US Army and later the 8th Supreme Allied Commander of NATO. XVIII-D-038

5 **LTG Winfield Scott:** USMA cadet gray uniforms come from his Battle of Chippewa victory. XXVII-A-016

6 **LTG James Gavin (USMA, 1929):** "Jumpin' Jim" was the youngest Division Commander in Europe during WWII. Served as ambassador to France under President Kennedy. X-M-36

7 **LTG Ying-Hsing Wen (USMA, 1909):** Admitted to USMA by a special act of Congress as first Chinese cadet. First Asian USMA graduate. XXVII-F-218

8 **MG John Buford (USMA, 1848):** Distinguished and meritorious service at the Battle of Gettysburg. XXVI-A-006

9 **MG Robert Anderson (USMA, 1825):** Commander of Fort Sumter at the start of the Civil War. The fountain by the cemetery caretaker's cottage is a memorial to him. XXVII-A-004

10 **MG George Goethals (USMA, 1880):** Oversaw the construction and the opening of the Panama Canal. XVIII-G-082

11 **MG Ethan Allen Hitchcock (USMA, 1817):** "Pen of the Army." A recognized philosopher and published scholar. XXVII-A-007

12 **MG George Sykes (USMA, 1842):** Division Commander during the Second Battle of Bull Run; thwarted enemy attempts to take Little Round Top during the Battle of Gettysburg. XXVI-A-001

13 **MG Wesley Merritt (USMA, 1860):** Distinguished officer during the Civil War and the Spanish-American War. XXII-A-009

14 **MG Daniel Butterfield:** Medal of Honor recipient and composer of the bugle call, "Taps." His monument is the most ornate in the cemetery and it documents thirty-eight battles and engagements of his career. XV-D-050

15 **BG Sylvanus Thayer (USMA, 1808):** Fifth West Point Superintendent and known as the "Father of West Point." XXV-A-022

16 **BG John Thompson (USMA, 1882):** Distinguished service in the Spanish American War and World War I. Inventor of the Thompson Submachine "Tommy" Gun. XIII-A-038

17 **BG Egbert Viele (USMA, 1847):** The Chief Engineer who oversaw the development of New York's Central Park. XXIV-F-259

18 **COL David "Mickey" Marcus (USMA, 1924):** Served with distinction during the 1948 Arab-Israeli War, then was recruited to become Israel's first modern general and was the Commander of Jerusalem. VI-B-125

19 **LTC George Armstrong Custer (USMA, 1861):** Served as a Brevet Major General during the Civil War, was a distinguished cavalryman up until his *Last Stand* at the Battle of Little Big Horn. XXVII-A-001

20 **LTC Edward White II (USMA, 1952):** First American to walk in space; posthumously awarded the Congressional Space Medal of Honor. XVIII-G-080

21 **1LT Laura Walker (USMA, 2003):** First female graduate killed in action. Fel in Afghanistan in 2005. XXVI-B-064C

22 **ENS Dominick Trant:** Buried in 1782, his headstone is the oldest grave marker in the cemetery. XXX-H-317

23 **MSGT Martin Maher:** Rose from the ranks of a civilian dishwasher, enlisted and completed a fifty year career at West Point. His story is told in the book "Bringing Up The Brass" and in the movie "The Long Gray Line" (1955). XIII-E-174

24 **Earl "Red" Blaik (USMA, 1920):** Served as USMA Head Football Coach with a 166-48-14 record. Led the 1944 and 1945 National Championship teams and coached three Heisman Trophy winners. X-G-131

25 **Margaret Corbin:** Heroine of the American Revolution. When her husband fell in battle, she took his position at the cannon during the defense of Fort Washington. XI-A-001

26 **Susan & Anna Warner:** Both sisters resided on Constitution Island prior to willing the land to the Academy; Susan wrote the well-known children's song "Jesus Loves Me, This I Know." XXX-Q-586-587

* SECTION-ROW-BURIAL PLOT

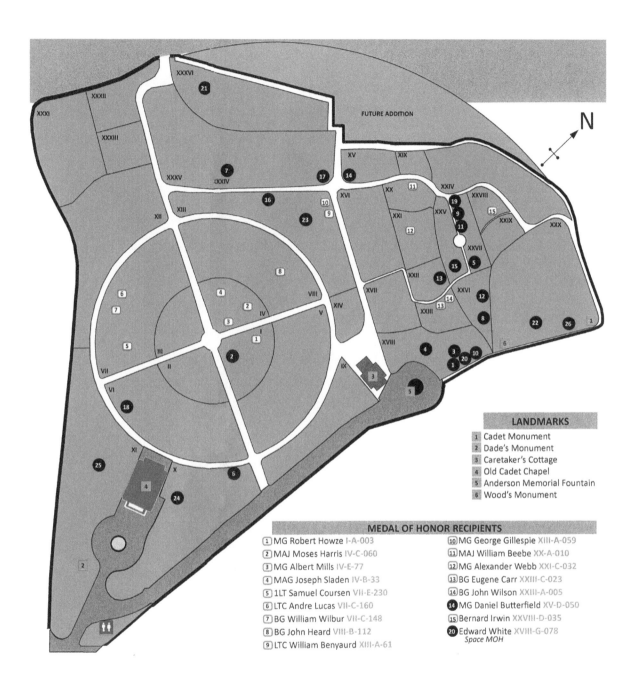

N

FUTURE ADDITION

LANDMARKS

1 Cadet Monument
2 Dade's Monument
3 Caretaker's Cottage
4 Old Cadet Chapel
5 Anderson Memorial Fountain
6 Wood's Monument

MEDAL OF HONOR RECIPIENTS

1 MG Robert Howze I-A-003
2 MAJ Moses Harris IV-C-060
3 MG Albert Mills IV-E-77
4 MAG Joseph Sladen IV-B-33
5 1LT Samuel Coursen VII-E-230
6 LTC Andre Lucas VII-C-160
7 BG William Wilbur VII-C-148
8 BG John Heard VIII-B-112
9 LTC William Benyaurd XIII-A-61

10 MG George Gillespie XIII-A-059
11 MAJ William Beebe XX-A-010
12 MG Alexander Webb XXI-C-032
13 BG Eugene Carr XXIII-C-023
14 BG John Wilson XXIII-A-005
14 MG Daniel Butterfield XV-D-050
15 Bernard Irwin XXVIII-D-035
20 Edward White XVIII-G-078
    Space MOH

THE WEST POINT CEMETERY

On the wind-swept plains high above the Hudson River, the cemetery at West Point has a long history. It served as a burial ground for early residents of the area and then Revolutionary War soldiers before 1817--the year it became an official military cemetery. Until that year, small burial plots scattered about the grounds served as places of interment. Over years of excavations and construction, those graves were moved to their present sites. In 1840, an improved road to the area was built, and a caretaker's cottage, still in use, was added in 1872.

Caretaker Cottage

The grounds encompass fourteen acres and feature a wide variety of trees: magnificent willows, Russian elms, and the rare Ginkgo tree among them. Over 9,000 individuals are buried here and, with little space left for future interments, the site will soon be filled. There are plans to expand the cemetery north along the bluff overlooking the Hudson.

Graves can be found from each of America's wars, and include those killed by arrows, musket balls, Viet Cong ambush, space capsule fire, improvised explosive devices, accidents, and natural deaths. Counted among the dead are fifteen Medal of Honor winners, and more than twenty former superintendents of the Academy. There is no designated walking tour of the grounds, nor is there a special criteria for the placement of graves; cadets are buried beside generals.

Wherever one walks, well-known names from the nation's past leap out.

These individuals, many of them rivals in life, lie united in final rest awaiting the ultimate trumpet call to sound. Their graves, so peaceful in the tree-lined groves high above the Hudson River, contrast with the tragic and sometimes violent deaths of many here. It is fitting that these leaders with glory-filled laurels to their names have found tranquility at the institution that was so vital to their lives, and to the nation they gallantly served.

To do honor to all buried here would take an encyclopedic work, as many have had volumes written on their careers. This book highlights the careers of some of the most famous, but then pauses to consider--as one will do when wandering the grounds--those whose lives and passing would be unheralded.

THE CADET CHAPEL

Upon entering the grounds you will encounter one of the earliest buildings at the Academy, the Cadet Chapel. First built in 1837, it was originally located across from the current cadet library. The Chapel is not an imposing edifice, but a small Greek-style temple with four columns in front. Inside, the white, curved ceiling is supported by fluted pillars, with dark box pews lining the aisles. The windows are white-shuttered with rounded tops, two being closed to serve as flag cases. Black memorial tablets are embedded in the walls in tribute to Revolutionary War generals and graduates who fought in the Mexican War. Surprisingly, there is a marker

for Benedict Arnold acknowledging his successful invasion of Canada and the skill displayed at Saratoga, the turning point of the Revolution. Because he betrayed the Continental cause in attempting to turn the fort at West Point over to the British, only Arnold's rank and birth date are on the tablet; the name has been omitted. Also found in the walls are early cannon, some captured from the British.

At the immediate front of the Chapel is a red velvet screen in front of which is an enclosed lectern and two side seats, all velvet-covered. The top of the screen is hung with draped flags surmounted by an eagle. Behind

Chapel Exterior

Chapel Interior

and above the screen is the eye-catching mural Peace and War, which was painted by Robert W. Weir, an instructor of drawing at the school from 1876 to 1883. On a star-splashed background are two figures leaning on a tablet which is inscribed, *"Righteousness exhalteth a nation, but sin is reproachful to any people"*. The figures are Peace, a dark skinned maiden clad in white holding an olive branch, and War, a Roman soldier with downcast eyes. Atop the tablet is an eagle astride a globe which gives the effect of great distance to the mural.

Near the front of the Chapel is the pew used by General Winfield Scott, America's foremost general between the Revolution and the Civil War. According to legend the pew was placed so that Scott could not be seen by the pastor and therefore comfortably snooze through warm summer services.

Directly above the entrance is a choir loft with a small pipe organ. Now electrified, the organ still has the old hand pump in place behind the pipe racks.

In 1910 it was suggested the Chapel be torn down to make room for a proposed construction project. Concerned cadets and graduates immediately raised $25,000 — quite a sum in those days — to relocate the Chapel to where it now stands. Since the Chapel's construction plans could not be found, it was dismantled brick by brick, under the direction of Lieutenant Colonel John M. Carson, and moved to the cemetery entrance.

EARLY GRAVES

ENSIGN DOMINICK TRANT
1764 ? - 1782
Not a Graduate

Trant is one of the many naturalized men of Irish ancestry buried in the cemetery. Little is known of his early life other than the fact he was born in Cork, Ireland, immigrated to the United States, and became a soldier in the Ninth Massachusetts Infantry. He arrived at West Point in 1782 at the age of 18, and was first buried near the present cadet library. His body was later moved to its present location, and is the oldest grave in the cemetery.

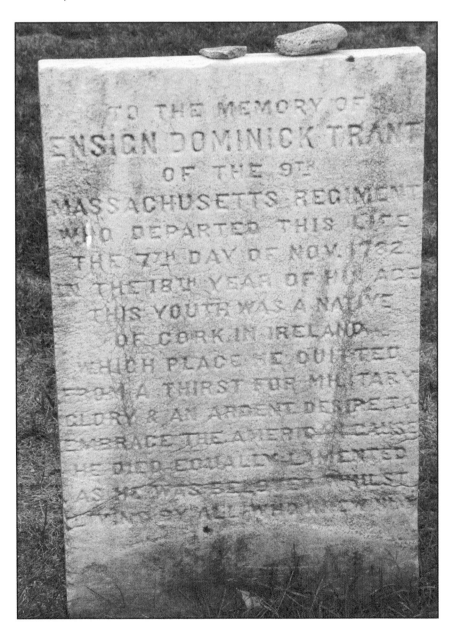

ROGER ALDEN
Captain, Continental Army
Not a Graduate

UNKNOWN

The graves of unknown individuals are located throughout the grounds; many are from the earliest days when bodies were relocated from other sites. The northeast section of the cemetery is the home of many unknowns— mostly Revolutionary War soldiers who had previously been scattered throughout the Academy grounds. Perhaps the saddest are the markers of unknown infants.

MARGARET 'MOLLY' CORBIN
1751-1800
Not a graduate

Margaret Molly Corbin was one of the first heroines of the newly formed United States. In those days wives would often accompany their husbands into campgrounds and a number actually took part in battles themselves. During the Battle of Fort Washington in New York, Molly took the place of her mortally wounded husband, working the cannon against advancing enemy troops until she herself was wounded. Washington took notice of her gallantry and arranged for her to receive a pension for life. A resident of Highland Falls, she was a colorful and controversial character and often petitioned West Point superintendents to buy her a new dress.

When the Daughters of the American Revolution certified her records in 1926, her remains were transferred from Highland Falls to the Academy's cemetery.

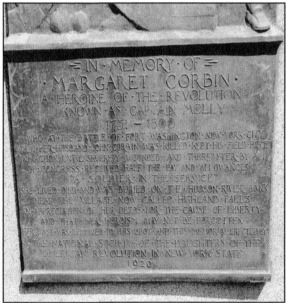

SYLVANUS THAYER
"Father of the Military Academy"
1785-1872
Class of 1808

Born in Braintree, Massachusetts, Thayer was educated at Dartmouth College before entering the Academy. Upon graduation he was assigned to the Corps of Engineers. Although still a lieutenant in 1812, Thayer was called into action as Chief Engineer to General Dear commanding the Niagara frontier. In 1813, he took command of Engineers in the Right Division of the Northern Army under General Hampton. Thayer was then ordered to Europe to study the operations of the Allied Armies operating against Paris as well as the military works and schools of European countries.

Thayer took his lessons learned to West Point when he became Superintendent in 1817, a position he held for the next sixteen years. Under his direction the academy became much more than an artillery school. West Point gained fame as the premier engineering school in the country. His cadets would go on to manage the building of most of the public works completed in the United States in the 19th century.

After a long-running dispute with President Jackson on the role of the Academy, Thayer was removed. He went on to other army duties including the construction of defenses for Boston harbor. His efforts to upgrade the Academy were so thorough and lasting that Sylvanus Thayer is justly regarded as the "Father of the Academy". He died in Braintree at the age of 87, the last of the Chiefs of Engineers from the War of 1812.

THE MEXICAN-AMERICAN WAR

When Mexico refused to recognize America's annexation of Texas and the Rio Grand River as the US-Mexican border in 1846, the United States went to war with Mexico. General Zachary Taylor (later President) and General Winfield Scott each led a major command of the American Army in the invasion of Mexico. Taylor won key battles at Monterrey and Buena Vista, while Scott's forces accomplished an amphibious landing at Veracruz and won a series of battles concluding with the capture of Mexico City on September 14, 1847. Scott was so impressed by the performance of West Point graduates that he recorded it was his "Fixed Opinion" that these officers were invaluable to the rapid and decisive nature of the US victory. Many of those junior officers later commanded Union and Confederate forces in the Civil War.

The U.S. lost 1,507 killed in combat, but eight times that number to disease, and over 4,000 wounded. Forty-eight West Point graduates were killed in action.

WINFIELD SCOTT
"Old Fuss and Feathers"
1786–1866
Not a Graduate

Surrounded by a wrought iron picket-style fence, the grave and memorial to Scott serve as a reminder of the nation's best general between the Revolution and the Civil War. While not a graduate of the Academy, the institution was dear to his heart in all the fifty-four years he served in the army.

During the War of 1812, Scott's command achieved victory when a British force of over twice their number mistook his regulars for militia. His experiences during the war proved him to be one of the country's ablest commanders.

In the 1840's the country was totally unprepared for war with Mexico. Early victories soon turned to stalemate when Scott stepped in to achieve one of the most brilliant victories of all military history. Going against the commonly held tenets of warfare, he abandoned his base of supplies and marched his army overland from the seacoast to Mexico City. In a series of actions and battles, his men marched into Mexico City itself, and all but ended the war.

After the war, while still in the army, Scott became actively involved in politics, but never achieved his dream of becoming President. The Civil War found him still in command of the American Army, but the responsibility was too great for the aging general. He remained at West Point throughout the war and lived to see his beloved country re-united.

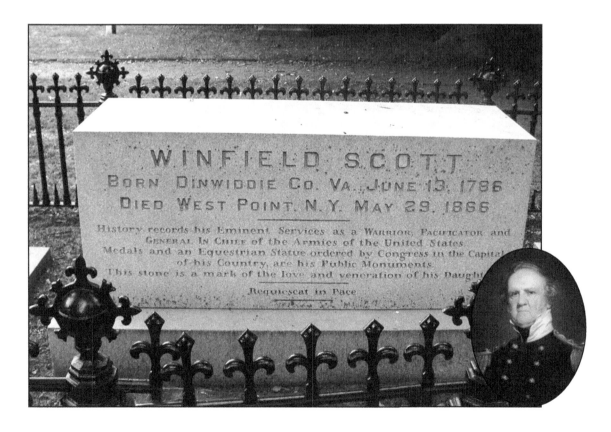

THE CIVIL WAR

The American Civil War (1861-1865) was fought over the secession of eleven southern slave states from the United States, forming the Confederate States of America. The remaining twenty-five states supported the federal government. It was the first truly industrial war utilizing the technologies developed in the first half of the century - railroads, telegraphs, and mass production of armaments. Pivotal battles in that war included Antietam, Vicksburg, Gettysburg, the Wilderness Campaign, Sherman's March to the Sea, and the siege at Petersburg.

Almost three quarters of a million combatants perished, including sixty West Pointers fighting for the Union and twenty-five fighting for the Confederacy. Twenty two West Pointers and two former cadets were awarded the Medal of Honor.

The following Civil War Generals are buried in this cemetery:

Anderson, Robert	MacKenzie, Ranald S.
Butterfield, Daniel	Merritt, Wesley
Buford, John	Neill, Thomas E.
Carr, Eugene	Newton, John
Custer, George A.	Ruger, Thomas H.
Gillmore, Quincy A.	Scott, Winfield S.
Groyer, Cuvier	Sykes, George
Hartsuff, George L.	Stone, Charles P.
Hays, William	Terrill, William R.
Hitchcock, Ethan Allen	Viele, Egbert
Jackson, William	Vogdes, Israel
Keyes, Erasmus D.	Webb, Alexander
Kilpatrick, Hugh J.	Wood, Thomas J.

All served the Union cause. No West Point graduate who served the Confederacy during the American Civil War is buried here.

ROBERT ANDERSON
1805-1871
Class of 1825

Robert Anderson took part in the Black Hawk War, the Seminole Indian Wars in Florida, and the war with Mexico.

As secession loomed, Anderson was assigned to command federal forts in Charleston, South Carolina harbor. When Confederate batteries fired on Fort Sumter in April 1861, he was able to defend the fortification for a time, but there was no hope for either victory or aid. His surrender was conditional upon his being able to leave the installation with colors flying and drums beating. In the North he became the first hero of the war.

He was promoted to brigadier general, and posted to Kentucky where he helped keep that pivotal state in the Union. Soon his health, both physical and mental, came under the strain, and he was relieved from duty and retired in October 1861. In 1865 he was breveted a major general and sent back to Fort Sumter to raise the same United States flag that had flown when he vacated the post.

THE ANDERSON FOUNTAIN

JOHN BUFORD
1826-1863
Class of 1848

Born in Woodford County , Kentucky , John Buford received his appointment to West Point in 1844. The young officer would see action throughout the western plains before the Civil War.

In August, 1862, Buford's horsemen attacked Confederates at Cedar Mountain, Kelly's Ford, Thoroughfare Gap, and Second Bull Run. In this last battle he was badly wounded while screening the rear of Pope's army. He returned to active command in1863 to lead the newly formed First Cavalry Division. His unit took part in the battle of Brandy Station in which the Union Cavalry finally matched that of the Confederacy.

At Gettysburg, Buford, portrayed by actor Sam Elliott in the 1993 movie epic, played a key role in the Union victory. When Confederate forces advanced on Gettysburg in the summer of 1863, Buford's greatly outnumbered cavalry halted them on the first day. During the night of June 30 to July 1, his division held off invading forces until the bulk of northern forces could be brought up. On July 1st, with almost no rest, his men continued to hold the ground that would be the key to Union victory.

Failing health, due to his earlier wounds, forced Buford to take leave of his command in November 1863. He went to the home of fellow officer and friend General George Stoneman in Washington, D.C. In December 16, 1863, lying on his deathbed, Buford received his commission as major general. His monument in the cemetery was purchased with funds raised by his soldiers.

EGBERT LUDOVICUS VIELE
1825–1902
Class of 1847

Viele was born in New York State, where his father had been a state senator and a judge. Upon his graduation from West Point, he was ordered to the war in Mexico, and then to frontier service.

Viele resigned his commission in 1853 and opened an office as a civil engineer in New York City. While the architect of the Central Park works, he began his study of the topography of Manhattan, calling attention to the idea of using the land's natural drainage system for the planning of streets and sewers. His book, *Topographical Atlas of the City of New York*, is still referred to by engineers today because of its insights on constructing large buildings.

Viele's monument is one of the most interesting on the grounds. Why he chose an Egyptian style monument complete with menacing Sphinx and two stone sarcophaguses for himself and his wife is unknown. However, Viele had a fear of being buried alive and had a buzzer installed inside the building. The wire ran to the caretaker's house where Viele could alert him if he awoke and somehow managed to get out of his stone coffin. The buzzer has since been removed.

DANIEL BUTTERFIELD
1831-1901
Not a graduate

Daniel Butterfield has been called the "fightingest" general from New York State in the Civil War. He was the type of leader who constantly pushed forward and hated to back up.

Serving as chief of staff to General Joseph Hooker, Butterfield held together the Army of the Potomac after the bitter defeats of Fredericksburg and Chancellorsville. Although he preferred combat, Butterfield, like Lucius Clay of World War II, was a master of logistics -- critical to every successful army in history. Still, he managed to participate in 28 battles and 15 skirmishes. For his contributions and valor, Congress awarded him the Medal of Honor.

During the war, Butterfield wrote the manual, *Camp and Outpost Duty*, which was widely used for its health and sanitary regulations. Butterfield initiated the use of shoulder patches for uniforms and cap insignias so units could be more easily identified. He is best remembered for his composition of Taps.

Butterfield was sent home ill with fever on June 29, 1864. After leaving the army, he became a successful railroad official. His memorial, nicknamed the Wedding Cake, is made of white marble. It is 25 feet wide with 16 ornate columns to record the 45 battles in which he participated.

ALONZO CUSHING
1841-1863
Class of 1861

Cushing, a native of Delafield, Wisconsin, was raised in Fredonia, New York, and graduated from the Academy June 1861. Commanding Battery A, 4th U.S. Artillery at Gettysburg on July 3, Cushing faced Picket's Charge at the Bloody Angle. Wounded twice and unable to stand, Cushing refused to fall back. He advanced his remaining guns toward the Confederates while being supported by 1st Sergeant, Frederick Füger. Shortly thereafter, Cushing was killed by a bullet through his mouth at the High Watermark of the Confederacy.

In a 1908 memoir, *The Spirit of Old West Point*, Morris Schaff, Class of 1862, wrote of his own experience as a cadet candidate:

Cushing fastened his eye upon me and then asked, his prominent white teeth gleaming through the radiant smile, "What's your name, Animal?" the title given by third-classmen to all new cadets,"

"Schaff," I answered demurely.

"Come right down here, Mr. Shad", commanded Cushing.

Well, I went and had the usual guying and subsequently was conducted to a room...where I was ordered to debate the repeal of the Missouri Compromise with another animal.

.....and years later...

I stayed over a month at Gettysburg after the battle, collecting and shipping the arms and guns left on the field - there were 37,574 muskets - and more than once I stood where brave Cushing gave his life, right at the peak of Pickett's daring charge. Oh, that day and hour! History will not let that smiling, splendid boy die in vain; long her dew will glisten over his record as the early morning dew glistens in the fields. ...

The dew still glistens on Cushing's record. He was nominated for the Medal of Honor in 2002. Because of the extended passage in time, this required an act Congress for approval which has not yet been granted.

HUGH JUDSON KILPATRICK
1836-1881
Class of 1861

Kilpatrick was born near Deckertown, New Jersey, the son of a farmer, and received a common school education prior to his admission to the Academy. He was graduated a year early to serve in the Civil War.

On June 10, 1861, he was severely wounded at the battle of Big Bethel. His actions won him promotion to lieutenant colonel in the Second New York Cavalry. For two years he took part in cavalry actions of the Army of the Potomac. On June 13, 1863, he was appointed brigadier general and took command of a division of cavalry that saw action at Aldie, Middleburg, and Upperville, Virginia. His men also took part in the fighting at Gettysburg. Though a successful commander, he was under constant criticism for his recklessness and seeming disregard for casualties. He bore the nickname "Kill Cavalry."

Kilpatrick resigned from the army at the war's conclusion and entered Republican politics. From 1865 - 68 he served as ambassador to Chile. One of his two daughters married into the Morgan banking family, the other into the Vanderbilt family. His granddaughter would be Gloria Vanderbilt.

37

THE INDIAN WARS

These were a series of conflicts between Native Americans, American settlers, and the US Army as settlements spread south and west across the continent between 1819 and 1890. The longest and costliest in lives lost was the Second Seminole War fought between 1835 and 1842. During the American Civil War, Army units were withdrawn to fight the war in the east, but returned with the resumption of the western expansion after 1865. Most of the fighting took place in the states bordering Mexico, with Arizona having the largest number of battles and casualties.

According to Army records, military personnel and civilians accounted for approximately 6,500 deaths while Indian casualties totaled about 15,000 during this period. Twenty-one USMA graduates were awarded the Medal of Honor.

THE DADE MEMORIAL

Erected in 1845, this cenotaph is a tribute to Brevet Major Francis L. Dade and his command massacred by Seminole Indians on a march to Fort King, Florida in 1835. The memorial is now located near the cemetery entrance, however its original site was near the Hudson River as depicted in an early post card issued by the NY Central Railroad.

ALEXANDER R. THOMPSON
1793-1837
Class of 1812

The inscription on this monument reads:

"Fell Dec 25, 1837 at the head of his regiment in a successful charge Battle of Okee-Cho-Bee Florida."

This was a major battle in the Second Seminole War fought over Seminole resistance to a forced relocation to the west. About 800 troops of regular infantry and 132 Missouri Volunteers battled about 450 Seminoles to draw on Christmas Day. The Seminoles had solid defensive positions and inflicted far more casualties on the soldiers than they incurred themselves. In the language of the official dispatch, Thompson

"received two balls from the fire of the enemy early in the action, which wounded him severely, yet; he appeared to disregard them, and continued to give his orders with the same coolness that he would have done had his regiment been under review, or any other parade duty. Advancing, he received a third ball, which at once deprived him of life: his last words were, 'Keep steady, men; charge the hammock -remember the regiment to which you belong.'

Colonel Zachary Taylor, commanding the Missouri Volunteers, was promoted to Brigadier General following battle and earned the nickname "Old Rough and Ready."

GEORGE ARMSTRONG CUSTER
1839-1876
Class of 1861

The third youngest brigadier general of the Civil War, and the second youngest major general in all United States history (only Lafayette was younger), Custer blazed a trail of glory that was both masterful and daring. Where there was action, there was Custer. His tragic death left unfulfilled a brilliant future.

A large book would be needed to describe this cavalry leader's career, and hundreds have been written. He was a man of volcanic energy. Like a comet he blazed brilliantly across the nation's sky, and like a comet his life ended in a flash in the Little Big Horn Valley in Montana. At the age of 36 he had met his destiny. Today, he and his wife Libbie rest side by side united in death in a lovely spot shaded by trees, a small area as tranquil in peace as his death was violent in battle.

Custer's war record is almost that of the war itself. At 23 his accomplishments were recognized, and he was promoted to brigadier general at the urging of Chief of Cavalry General Alfred Pleasanton. Within a few days he justified this action by winning a sweeping victory with his famed Michigan Brigade over General J.E.B.Stuart at Hanover, PA just east

of Gettysburg. During the course of the war, 11 horses were shot from under him with but one wound to himself. Appomattox found his glory-laden Third Division hounding the retreating Army of Northern Virginia, and it was Custer who would receive Lee's flag of surrender. General Phil Sheridan was so grateful to Custer that he purchased the table on which Lee signed the surrender, and gave it as a gift to Custer's wife with a note stating that he knew of no man who had done so much as her husband to bring that moment on; a remarkable tribute from such a great leader in his own right.

Taking command of the newly formed Seventh Cavalry after the war, Custer won the Army's first large victory against the hostile Indians at the Washita in 1868. In 1873 the unit was again victorious in the Yellowstone Campaign, and in 1874 the Seventh opened the Black Hills to the nation. Custer led the Seventh in its journey to destiny at the Little Big Horn in Montana in 1876. His immediate command of five companies with over 200 men would go into battle and never return.

ELIZABETH BACON CUSTER
1842–1933
Not a Graduate.

Born into a well-to-do family of Monroe, Michigan, Elizabeth Bacon was courted by a young Captain Custer and became his biggest booster. She accompanied Custer on many of his Civil War campaigns. Of all the officer's wives, it was only Libbie whom General Sheridan permitted near the front for she never complained or caused trouble.

After the war, Libbie was her husband's constant companion in deserts, plains, thirst and hunger, never losing her sense of humor or perspective. After the Battle of the Little Big Horn in 1876, Libbie would become the custodian of her husband's memory, and defended his reputation with all in her power. She became a noted businesswoman and popular writer. Her book *Boots and Saddles* is one of the finest works ever produced about army life. She survived her husband by over a half century.

CHARLES BRADEN
1847-1919
Class of 1869

When only 13 years old, Charles Braden took a rifle and tried to join the army. As an 1869 academy graduate, he left the Academy too late to take part in the Civil War. Braden was commissioned a second lieutenant in the Seventh Cavalry in 1869, under the command of Lieutenant Colonel George Armstrong Custer.

During the regiment's victorious Yellowstone Campaign of 1873 Braden's thigh was shattered by a bullet in a fight with the Sioux Indians. The wound was so bad that he had to be carried on a litter for 400 miles to the base of supply, and then on to Fort Abraham Lincoln in present day North Dakota. One of Custer's favorite officers, Braden would find his career largely terminated by the wound.

In 1878 he was forced to retire for health reasons and then taught in private schools before going on to a career in manufacturing. He is just an example of one of the many hundreds of cadets who showed tremendous promise, but had their careers cut short in service of their country.

RANALD SLIDELL MacKENZIE
1840-1889
Class of 1862

Born in New York City, Ranald MacKenzie went to Williams College before withdrawing to enter West Point, where he graduated in 1861 number one in his class. He took part in the battles of Manassas, Fredericksburg, Chancellorsville, Gettysburg, the Wilderness, Spotsylvania, and the siege of Petersburg. Tenacity and bravery earned him promotion to major general of volunteers. His cavalry division was instrumental in the victories at Five Forks and Appomattox.

After the war, he was transferred to the southwestern frontier and engaged in many Indian campaigns. In 1871 he was severely wounded while fighting in Texas. After the Custer fight in Montana, General Sheridan brought MacKenzie with six companies of the Fourth Cavalry to Nebraska to form a section of the Powder River Expedition against the Sioux and Cheyenne. On November 25, 1876, he located the Cheyenne in the Big Horn Mountains and shattered the tribe of Chief Dull Knife in battle. This action, coupled with the success of Colonel Nelson Miles in Montana, led to the surrender of Crazy Horse.

The Army knew when it had a good Indian fighter, and MacKenzie was transferred back to Texas where he pacified the region down to the Rio Grande. In 1879 he was transferred to deal with the Ute Indian outbreaks in Utah and Colorado. MacKenzie's reports were simple and concise, lacking any element of self-promotion. His total aversion to publicity has left his achievements unheralded.

MacKenzie retired in March 1888 because of failing health and died a year later in Staten Island, New York. Little known, MacKenzie was a superb officer in the finest traditions of the American Army.

THE SPANISH-AMERICAN WAR

The Spanish–American War was a brief but far-flung war in 1898 between Spain and the United States.   By 1897–98, American public opinion was incensed at reports of Spanish atrocities in Cuba. After the mysterious sinking of the battleship Maine in Havana harbor in February 1898, the American press howled for justice. President William McKinley was compelled to enter a war which he thought unwise. When an ultimatum demanding that Spain immediately surrender control of Cuba was rejected by the Spanish, war ensued.

The seventy-five day war was fought in both the Caribbean and the Pacific. American naval power provided a decisive edge, allowing U.S. expeditionary forces to disembark in Cuba and the Philippines. U.S. forces soon triumphed. The resulting treaty gave temporary control of Cuba to the United States. Additionally, Spain agreed to sell its interests in Puerto Rico, Guam, and the Philippines to the United States, inciting a national debate about America's role as a colonial power.

The United States suffered just over 2,446 battle deaths.   Sixteen West Pointers died in the conflict and four were awarded the Medal of Honor.

WESLEY MERRITT
1836-1910
Class of 1860

Today the accomplishments of Wesley Merritt are overshadowed by his contemporary George A. Custer. This is unfortunate, for Merritt was one of the finest officers ever produced by the United States. During the Civil War he was promoted on six occasions, eventually becoming the Superintendent of West Point, and then commanding United States forces in the Philippines. His was a brilliant military career.

In 1862 he was promoted to captain in the Second Cavalry, then the best in the Union forces. He took part in the Stoneman raid toward Richmond in 1863, and was then promoted to the staff of General Alfred Pleasanton; soon after he was promoted to brigadier general. During the third day at Gettysburg his command won distinction near little Round Top. Shortly after he was promoted to major general and given charge of the Second Division of Cavalry under Sheridan. At Yellow Tavern, joining Custer's forces, the Union routed the cavalry of J.E.B. Stuart, who was killed in the fray. Like Custer, Merritt spent the rest of the war serving under Sheridan where both had splendid records and became rivals for the laurels of glory.

Following the Civil War, he was posted west for the upcoming Indian campaigns. In 1882 he was appointed Superintendent of West Point, and for the next five years concentrated on raising the admission requirements. From 1887 until 1897, he headed both the East and Missouri Departments of the army.

With the commencement of the Spanish-American War, Merritt was given the choice of leading an invasion of Cuba or the Philippines. He chose the far more difficult assignment to the Far East, which involved the largest movement of United States troops to that time taking 20,000 men over 7,000 miles into battle. Returning to the states, he resumed command of the Department of the East until his retirement a year later.

FREDERICK DENT GRANT
1850-1912
Class of 1871

Son of General U.S.Grant, Frederick was born in St. Louis, Missouri. During the Civil War he often accompanied his father in the field where he saw considerable action. At Vicksburg he suffered a bullet wound, and later contracted an illness that proved almost fatal. Upon his graduation from West Point he sought adventure serving on the frontier, often with Custer.

In 1878-79 young Grant accompanied the former President's world tour. He resigned from the army in 1881, but rejoined in 1898 to serve in the Spanish-American War. Later he commanded units in the Philippines operating against the insurgents.

Returning to the United States with the permanent rank of brigadier general, Grant took charge of the Department of Texas. In 1906 he was promoted to major general.

JOSHUA FOWLER
1846-1899
Class of 1868

Major Fowler died at sea return-ing from Cuba, July 1899.

DENNIS MAHAN MICHIE
1870–1898
Class of 1892

Michie coached West Point's first football team while still a cadet in 1890. He accepted a challenge from the midshipmen from Annapolis, and the Greatest Game in college football was born. He was killed at the Battle of San Juan Hill in 1898. The Army Black Knights play their home football games in Michie Stadium.

PHILIPPINE INSURRECTION

This conflict between U.S. troops and Filipino revolutionaries followed the close of the Spanish American War with the annexation of the Philippines by the United States,   Many Filipinos felt betrayed by the United States in denying them independence after centuries of Spanish rule. Fighting erupted in February, 1899, and escalated into the full-scale Battle of Manila. The ferocious guerilla war, replete with atrocities on both sides, was brought to a close in on July 4, 1902 after the capture of Aguinaldo and the most prominent Filipino generals. Following World War II, the United States granted full independence to the territory.

U.S. deaths amounted to just over 2,400, including 22 West Pointers. Nine West Pointers were awarded the Medal of Honor for actions in the Philippines.

GEORGE GODFREY
1862-1900
Class of 1886

THOMAS CONNELL
1872-1901
Class of 1894

Captain Godfrey was killed in action at San Miguel, Philippines on June 3, 1900.

Captain Connell's memorial notes that he served with the 9th U.S Infantry in Cuba, China, and the Philippines. He was killed in action at San Balanciga Samar, Philippines on Sept 28, 1901.

MEXICO BORDER CAMPAIGN

The Border Campaign (1910-1919) encompassed a series of engagements along the Mexican-American boundary during the Mexican Revolution. The U.S. Army, stationed along the border to protect American citizenry, occasionally engaged Mexican federal troops or rebels. The most notable event occurred in 1916 when revolutionary Pancho Villa attacked the American border town of Columbus, New Mexico. In response, the United States Army, under the direction of General John J. Pershing, launched an expedition into northern Mexico to find and capture Villa. Failing to capture Villa, the American army returned to the United States in January 1917. Conflict at the border continued however and the United States launched several more smaller operations into Mexican territory until 1919.

JO WEBSTER ALLISON Jr.
1890-1916
Class of 1914

WORLD WAR I

The United States was a neutral party for most of World War I (at that time known as "The Great War"), but was finally drawn into war, principally by Germany's unrestricted submarine war policy. The tipping point was the Zimmerman Telegram from the German Foreign Minister inviting Mexico into an alliance for Germany's support in returning the states of the American Southwest to Mexico. Scrambling to mobilize the Army, the U.S quickly deployed naval forces to support the Allies, sending an Expeditionary Force to France in late 1917. By mid-1918 the Army was sending hundreds of thousands of troops per month to Europe. American forces turned the tide in favor of the Allies. An Armistice was signed on November 11, 1918.

Over 117,000 Americans were killed in the War, thirty-two of them West Pointers. Of the 119 Americans who received the Medal of Honor for action in World War I, only one attended West Point.

Two West Pointers who achieved renown in World War I, John Pershing and Douglas MacArthur, are buried elsewhere. Several thousand younger officers served with distinction and went on to leadership positions in the Second World War.

WALTER GALLAGHER
1880-1918
Class of 1903

EDWARD ROSSELL
1895-1918
Class of 1917

WALTER H. SCHULZE
1893-1919
Class of 1917

The irony of Captain Shulze's death is etched on his tombstone. He had just completed his assignment to fly the news that the Great War was over to units east of the Rhine. On the way home, his plane crashed and he was killed.

WORLD WAR II

The Second World War (1939 - 1945) involved the majority of the world's nations—including all of the great powers—in two opposing military alliances, the Allies and the Axis. It resulted in 50 to 70 million fatalities, making it the deadliest conflict in all of human history.

By 1941 Germany had conquered or controlled the European continent. Aligning with the Axis of Germany and Italy, Japan set upon dominating East Asia and Indochina. In December 1941 the Japanese attacked the United States and Great Britain at Pearl Harbor, the Philippines, Indochina, and Malaysia, quickly conquering much of the western Pacific.

The Axis advance was stopped in 1942 after Japan lost a series of naval battles to the U.S. Navy, while in Europe Axis forces were defeated in North Africa and decisively at Stalingrad in the winter of 1943. In June 1944, the U.S forces and western Allies invaded France, while the Soviet Union regained all of its territorial losses and set upon Germany. The war in Europe ended with the capture of Berlin by Soviet troops and the subsequent German unconditional surrender in May 1945. During 1944 and 1945 the United States routed the Japanese Navy, capturing key Pacific archipelagoes and the Philippines. Faced with the invasion of the Japanese home islands and the prospects of a staggering loss of life, President Truman approved the dropping of atomic bombs on Hiroshima and Nagasaki in August 1945. Japan promptly capitulated and the war ended with the surrender ceremony in Tokyo Bay on September 2, 1945.

The United States suffered just over 405,000 deaths, 487 of them West Point graduates. The largest number of West Pointers perished in the Army Air Force. Flying and flight training were exceptionally perilous. Nine USMA graduates and one former cadet were awarded the Medal of Honor.

LUCIUS D. CLAY
1897-1978
Class of 1918

Lucius D. Clay is one of the very few generals of any army to receive four star rank without holding a combat command. When World War II began Clay hungered for combat, but the army could not spare his genius for logistics. With the invasion of mainland Europe in 1944, harbors were not being re-opened at the anticipated pace. General Dwight D. Eisenhower asked Clay to take on the near-hopeless task of rebuilding Cherbourg, France. For his leadership in the rapid reconstruction of the port facilities he was awarded the Bronze Star.

After the war Eisenhower placed Clay in charge of all civil affairs in war-ravaged Germany. Joseph Stalin, the Soviet dictator, decided to force the Allies out of the city of West Berlin, which lay in the heart of the Soviet sector of Germany, by blockading all land routes to the city. Stalin received a harsh lesson in Allied will-power from General Clay. This tough-minded officer organized what became known as the Berlin Airlift. During the year-long Soviet blockade of 1948-1949, Clay supervised the flying in of 2,343,315 tons of food and clothing saving Berliners from starvation and keeping the city free. Almost every aircraft available to of the United States was used in this monumental endeavor.

Returning to the United States in 1949, Clay was given a hero's welcome with a tickertape parade in New York City and decorated by President Truman.

58

JAMES GAVIN
1907–1990
Class of 1929

Gavin enlisted in the Army at the age of 17 and earned his appointment to West Point within a year. Throughout his schooling and career he was a persistent and inquisitive scholar, especially of military tactics and strategy.

He avoided lengthy written orders by giving rough guidelines for the commanders in the field to execute, employing their own initiative and resourcefulness.

When he took command of the 82nd Airborne Division during World War II, he was the youngest major general commanding a division since the American Civil War.

Gavin was referred to as "the jumping general", insisting that officers be "the first out of the airplane door and the last in the chow line." During combat, he usually carried an M1 Garand rifle instead of the traditional pistol carried by staff officers.

After the war Gavin stimulated military doctrine discussions of a modern "cavalry" in lightweight armored vehicles and helicopters. This led to the Army's adoption of helicopters for rapid troop and materiel movements, first widely used during the Viet Nam War.

Gavin retired from the Army in 1958 as a Lieutenant General and served as the United States ambassador to France from 1961–63.

FRANK DOW MERRILL
1903–1955
Class of 1929

Frank Merrill was notable for his persistence. Graduating from high school in 1921, he was rejected for admission to West Point because of astigmatism. Undaunted, he enlisted in the regular army in 1922, while continuing to apply for admission to the Academy. After five separate rejections he was finally admitted in 1925.

When the Japanese attacked Pearl Harbor, Merrill was in Rangoon, Burma. He joined the staff of Lieutenant General Joseph Stilwell in the China-Burma-India Theater. Merrill was with Stillwell when Burma fell, and started on the now famous walk out of the jungle to India. A heart attack caused him to collapse, and he had to be carried out on the final leg of the trek.

In December 1943, Stilwell launched his own offensive with two American-trained Chinese divisions into northern Burma. Merrill commanded the American troops, a unit that came to be called Merrill's Marauders, in spearheading the offensive. The Marauders accomplished bitterly hard marches through the mountains and tropical terrain. Struck down with another heart attack, Merrill had to be evacuated in March 1943, but continued his command into 1944.

After the war, Merrill settled in New Hampshire and designed that state's turnpike while doing other engineering work until his death.

Merrill and Stillwell in Burma

JOSEPH WARREN STILWELL
1883-1946
Class of 1904

Many historians regard Joseph Stilwell as one of the finest of all army officers, and certainly one of the most controversial. Rivaling General George S. Patton's controversial remarks in the European Theater, Stilwell was easily his match in the Pacific. He earned the nickname "Vinegar Joe" for his tart and sarcastic personal observations.

Born in Florida, Stilwell graduated from West Point in the class of 1904 and served with American forces in France during World War I, earning a reputation for efficiency, steadfastness, and pragmatism. Shortly after the war he was transferred to American units in China, later serving from 1935 to 1939 as a military attaché in Peking. When the government needed advice on how to deal with Japan's attack on China, he was recalled to the United States, but returned to China as a lieutenant general after Pearl Harbor. He was placed in command of the China-Burma-India theater, although he had virtually no troops to command.

Stillwell soon recognized that the head of the Chinese government, Chiang Kai Shek, was hoarding supplies meant to fight the Japanese, and accumulating them for his post-war struggle with the Communists. Stilwell later feuded with British Admiral Lord Mountbatten, who headed Allied forces in the CBI theater. His inability to compromise and insistance on directness and efficiency led to his recall to the United States.

In November 1944, he was made a full general and given command of the United States Army Ground Forces, in effect, a position designed to keep him out of the public eye for a time. In June 1945, he was given command of the Tenth Army in the Pacific, but the war ended in September. In October 1946, he died of cancer in San Francisco.

ALEXANDER M. PATCH
1889-1945
Class of 1913

Alexander Patch was the son of an Army officer stationed at Fort Huachuca, AZ. He wanted to be a cavalryman like his father, but chose infantry upon graduation from West Point, realizing that the days of the horse cavalry were ending.

During World War I, Patch served with distinction as an infantry officer and as an instructor, gaining the attention of George C. Marshall. Before World War II, Marshal promoted Patch to brigadier general and sent him to Fort Bragg to oversee the training of new soldiers.

Patch was promoted to major general in March 1942 and sent to the Southwest Pacific to organize the reinforcement and defense of New Caledonia. He commanded a collection of units, forming them into the Americal Division (a contraction of "American, New Caledonian Division"). It was later re-classified as the 23rd Infantry Division. Twenty years later it was revived for service in the Viet Nam war.

The Americal Division first saw action in the Guadalcanal campaign in October 1942, in relieving the valiant but malaria-ridden 1st Marine Division. In December 1942, Patch assumed command of the entire offensive on Guadalcanal and personally led troops on missions against Japanese forces. Under his leadership the Japanese were driven from Guadalcanal in February 1943.

General Marshall then ordered Patch to Europe to take command of the Seventh Army from General Mark Clark. The Seventh Army landed in southern France on 15 August 1944, after which Patch – now promoted to lieutenant general - led a fast offensive up the Rhone Valley. On 9 September 1944, near Dijon, France, the Seventh Army joined with elements of Lieutenant General George

S. Patton's Third Army that had driven east from the beaches of Normandy. Patch suffered a personal tragedy when his son, Captain Alexander M. Patch III, an infantry company commander, was killed in action on 22 October 1944.

Patch retained command of the Seventh Army through the end of the war, crossing the Siegfried Line and moving into southern Germany.

In August 1945, Patch returned to the United States to take command of the Fourth Army, but was hospitalized with lung problems. He died of pneumonia on 21 November 1945.

RICHARD O'CONNOR
Class of 1926
KIA in Sicily
July 1943

ROBERT M. LOSEY
Class of 1929
Captain Losey, military attaché, was killed by a German bomb during the Nazi invasion of Norway, the first U.S. officer to die as an act of war in that conflict.

SAMUEL CUMMINGS MITCHELL
Class of 1935
Air accident, El Paso TX
May 1943

HARRY FRANKLIN SELLERS
Class of 1935
Killed on Luzon, Philippines
January 1945

GEORGE BREITLING
Class of 1939
Japanese POW
January, 1945

CHARLES WHITE
Class of 1939
Japanese POW
September, 1944

CHARLES ANDREWS SPRAGUE
Class of 1937
MIA on an air mission over Java
February, 1942

MILFORD F. STABLEIN
Class of 1940
KIA Lorraine France
November, 1944

FRANK E. LOCKE
Class of 1941
Air Accident
August, 1942

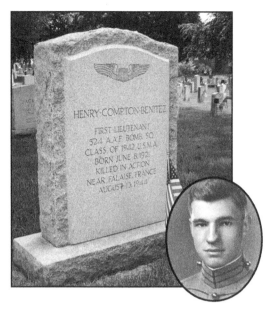

HENRY BENITEZ
Class of 1942
KIA at Falaise France
August, 1944

THOMAS F. FARRELL Jr.
Class of 1942
KIA at Anzio
February, 1944

FREDERIC HOMER TATE
Class of 1942
Air Mission, Vigneulles France
September, 1944

SAMUEL GIBSON Jr.
Class of 1942
KIA Rhineland
December, 1944

CHARLES HENRY COLWELL
Class of 1942
Air accident in India
June, 1943

HARRY R. STROH
Class of Jan 1943
Air Mission, Brest France
August, 1944

LAWTON DAVIS
Class of 1943
KIA Belgium
January, 1945

HARRY KENYON Jr.
Class of 1943
KIA The Rhineland
March, 1945

BENJAMIN NORRIS Jr.
Class of January 1943
Air accident
July, 1943

WOODROW WILSON PRATT
Class of 1943
KIA Germany
November, 1944

TURNER CHAMBLISS Jr.
Class of 1943
KIA D-Day
June 6, 1944

THE KOREAN WAR

Following the Japanese surrender in September 1945, the Korean peninsula was divided along the 38th parallel, with U.S. forces occupying the south and Soviet forces occupying the north. The North established a communist government, while the South established a capitalist one. Tensions intensified at the 38th parallel with skirmishes and raids. Finally, North Korean forces invaded South Korea in late June 1950, which became the major armed conflict of the Cold War. At the United Nations, taking advantage of a boycott by the Soviet Union, the United States led the Security Council in authorizing military intervention in Korea.

Over 20 countries allied with the United States, who provided almost 90% of the soldiers, aided South Korea in repelling the invasion. Within two months, suffering severe casualties, the Allies were pushed back to a small area in the south known as the Pusan perimeter. A rapid U.N. counter-offensive sparked by a remarkable amphibious invasion at Inchon near Seoul then drove the North Koreans back north past the 38th Parallel and almost to the Yalu River bordering the Chinese People's Republic. China then entered the war on the side of North Korea, forcing the Allied forces to retreat back below the 38th Parallel. The lines stabilized and the major hostilities ended with an armistice on July 27, 1953 at Panmunjom. The agreement restored the border between the Koreas near the 38th Parallel and created a fortified buffer zone between the two Korean nations. A peace treaty was never signed.

The U.S. lost over 36,000 killed in action, among them 157 West Point graduates. Two West Pointers received the Medal of Honor.

BRYANT E. MOORE
1904-1951
Class of 1917

Bryant Moore commanded troops on Guadalcanal in 1942. After promotion to general, he served as Deputy Commander of the 104th Infantry Division in Northern France, and later the 8th Infantry Division in Europe. With the end of the war in Europe he moved to command the occupation of Yugoslavia. Moore served as Superintendent at West Point from 1949 until 1951. He loved sailing and frequently cruised the Hudson River.

With the outbreak of the Korean War, he was called to Korea to command the IX Corps. Not long after his arrival General Moore's helicopter crashed on February 24, 1951. He died of an apparent heart attack after obtaining help for the pilot and crew. Moore was promoted to the rank of four-star general posthumously.

FRANK HOWZE
Class of 1941
KIA September, 1950

BOONE SEEGERS
Class of 1943
Army Air Force
KIA July, 1950

JOHN H. JONES
Class of 1945
KIA January, 1951

GEORGE WILLIAM TOW
Class of 1949
KIA September, 1950

WARNER T. BONFOEY Jr.
Class of 1950
KIA October, 1951

FRANK PETER CHRISTENSEN Jr.
Class of 1950
KIA October, 1951

ELLIOT REYNOLDS KNOTT
Class of 1950
Air Accident, Japan
December, 1951

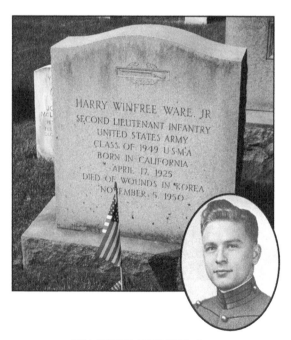

HARRY WARE Jr.
Class of 1949
KIA November, 1950

VIET NAM

The Viet Nam War was a Cold War conflict in Southeast Asia from 1955 to 1975. North Viet Nam, supported by communist allies was endeavoring to overthrow the government of South Viet Nam and unify the country. The United States and anti-communist countries came to the aid of the South Vietnamese government. A communist-supported South Vietnamese faction, the Viet Cong, conducted a guerrilla war against the government while the North Vietnamese Army engaged in larger unit actions. U.S. and South Vietnamese forces utilized air superiority and overwhelming firepower to combat the Communists in what came to be known as "search and destroy" operations.

U.S. involvement escalated in the early 1960s, moving from teams of advisors to the commitment of tens of thousands of troops following the Tonkin Bay incident in August 1964. Ultimately, the United States had more than a half million soldiers in Viet Nam with large naval and air forces in the region. American public opinion grew restive with this large commitment and ensuing losses in an impoverished land. The turning point came in January 1968, when the North Vietnamese staged the Tet Offensive throughout South Viet Nam. Though a military setback for the communists, it sparked U.S. public opinion against the war. Under a policy of "Vietnamization," U.S. ground forces were gradually withdrawn culminating in the Paris Peace Accords in January 1973. This did not stop the fighting. The Viet Nam People's Army captured Saigon in April 1975 ending the war and leading to reunification of the country in 1976.

The United States forces suffered over 58,000 combat deaths including 273 West Pointers. Eight West Pointers, including one former cadet and one professor, were awarded the Medal of Honor.

PAUL HARKINS
1904-1984
Class of 1929

During his career, Paul Harkins played a key role in several notable events in Army history. First, in World War II he served as the deputy Chief of Staff in Patton's Third Army as it drove towards Germany in an heroic diversion to relieve besieged Bastogne in the Battle of the Bulge.

Second, as commandant of cadets at West Point in 1950, Harkins was informed by a cadet that a group of cadets, mainly among the football team, were involved in a cheating ring. Disregarding the implications to the football team's national ranking, Harkins asked cadets to gather information about the cheating which led to a formal inquiry. As a result over ninety cadets were dismissed from the academy for violation of the Honor Code.

Finally, Harkins commanded the early build-up of American forces in Viet Nam - the Military Assistance Command Viet Nam (MACV) - during the Kennedy Administration. When he was succeeded by General Westmoreland June 1964, there were approximately 15,000 troops in Viet Nam. That later grew to over half a million by 1968.

WILLIAM WESTMORELAND
1914-2005
Class of 1936

A native of South Carolina, Westmoreland attended The Citadel in 1932 before receiving an appointment to West Point's Class of 1936 one that also included Creighton Abrams and Benjamin O. Davis Jr. Westmoreland graduated as first captain and branched to Field Artillery. During World War II he saw combat in Tunisia, Sicily, France and Germany, reaching the rank of brevet Colonel with the 82nd Airborne Division.

He then attended Harvard Business School and typified the new breed of Army officer with a managerial outlook. General James Gavin asked him to re-join the 82nd as a regimental commander. He served with that unit as a field commander for four years through the Korean War. In 1956, he became the youngest major general in the Army at the age of 42. In 1958 Westmoreland took command of the 101st Airborne Division and served as the Superintendent of West Point from 1960 to 1963.

In June 1964, he became deputy commander of Military Assistance Command, Viet Nam (MACV), assuming direct control from General Paul D. Harkins. As the head of the MACV he was known for highly publicized, positive assessments of US military prospects in Viet Nam. However, as time went on, the strengthening of communist combat forces in the South led to regular requests for increases in US troop strength, from less than 16,000 when he arrived to its peak of 535,000 in 1968.

Under Westmoreland's leadership, United States forces "won every battle." Nevertheless, public support at home and in Congress continued to erode. The 1968 Tet Offensive was the turning point. Political debate and public opinion led the Johnson administration to limit further increases in US troop numbers in Viet Nam and Johnson's decision to not seek re-election in 1968.

Westmoreland was promoted to Army Chief of Staff in June 1968, serving in that capacity until 1972 and his retirement from the Army.

JOHN STONEBURNER
Class of 1953

As an advisor to ARVN troops, he was killed in action by hostile fire near Tam Ky, Quang Tin Province, Dec 9, 1964.

WILLIAM TRAIN III
Class of 1959

As an advisor to ARVN troops, he was killed in action while on patrol in Binh Duong province, June 16, 1962, the sixth Army advisor to die in Viet Nam.

DEE STONE Jr.
Class of 1964

As a helicopter pilot serving with the 1-19 Field Artillery, he was killed in action November 11, 1966.

JERRY CLARK
Class of 1965

Serving with the 25th Infantry Division, fatally wounded June, 21, 1967, on a search and destroy mission in the booby-trapped tunnels of Duc Pho.

ROBERT ARVIN
Class of 1965

Lt. Arvin was serving as an advisor with the ARVN's 7th Airborne Battalion in Thua Thien province. On October 8,1967, they were completing a sweep of a suspected enemy base when it came under intense enemy fire leaving the unit pinned down. Lt. Arvin moved through the fire to a forward vantage point to direct gunship passes onto enemy positions. As he positioned himself to better direct the supporting fire, Arvin was mortally wounded. He was awarded the Silver Star for his selfless efforts. The gymnasium complex at West Point is named in his honor.

MICHAEL MOMCILOVICH Jr.
Class of 1965

Serving with the 1st Cavalry Division, killed in action on May 4, 1968 when the helicopter he was piloting was hit by hostile fire and crashed a few miles inland from the coast in Quang Tri Province.

GARY KADETZ
Class of 1965

Killed on 19 May 1966 by enemy fire during Operation "Wahiawa" while acting as a forward observer with Company A, 2d Battalion, 27th Infantry.

CHARLES WUERTENBERGER
Class of 1965

Killed in action January 17, 1968, when B Company, 2nd Battalion, 14th Infantry was ambushed by a large enemy force in Tay Ninh Province. He was awarded the Silver Star for gallantry in this action.

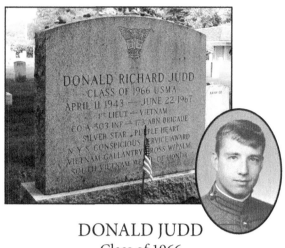

DONALD JUDD
Class of 1966

On 22 June 1967, serving with Company A, 2nd Battalion, 503rd Infantry Regiment, in Kontum Province, mortally wounded while rescuing fallen soldiers from his platoon who were pinned down by heavy automatic weapons. Awarded the Silver Star for gallantry.

WILLIAM D. BOOTH
Class of 1966

On 12 May 1970 serving as ADC to Major General Dillard, U.S. Army Engineer Command, Captain Booth was killed when the helicopter in which he was riding was shot down by enemy ground fire approximately twelve miles southeast of Pleiku. The general also died in the crash.

HUGH McKIBBIN Jr.
Class of 1966

Serving with the 2nd Battalion, 34th Infantry, 1st Infantry Division (The Big Red One) when he was killed in action on February 2, 1968 in Binh Duong province while attempting to rescue fallen comrades. Awarded the Silver Star for gallantry.

RICHARD THOMPSON
Class of 1966

Platoon leader "Buck" Thompson perished on November 19, 1967 with Company C, 2nd Battalion, 503rd Infantry in the horrific battle for Hill 875 in the Central Highlands. As the lead element established contact with the enemy fortifications, Lt. Thompson maneuvered his platoon into an assault line and pushed forward as it came under intense automatic weapons, rockets, and mortar fire. With little regard for his personal safety, he exposed himself to direct fire to guide his troops. As his platoon was moving into the company's defensive perimeter, Buck learned that his platoon sergeant was wounded and not with the platoon. Disregarding his own safety and already twice wounded himself, Buck returned to the contact area which was still receiving enemy mortar fire. He dragged his platoon sergeant back to safety. While in the process of reconsolidating the platoon's position, Buck was mortally wounded. He was awarded the Silver Star for gallantry.

CHARLES L. HEMMINGWAY
Class of 1965

As an infantry platoon commander with Adv Team 162 on a search and destroy mission in Thua Thien province on June 17, 1967, he was mortally wounded when a land mine exploded. While still conscious, Hemmingway calmly radioed to his senior advisor with details of the incident and asked to be med-evacuated. An hour later word came back that he had died.

WALLACE A. FORD III
Class of 1949

Lt. Colonel Ford USAF was flying an A-1H Skyraider for the 6th Air Command Squadron in support of ground operations on May 24, 1968 when he was shot down about 15 miles west of Tam Ky in Quang Tri province.

JOHN A. KEMP
Class of 1961

BLACKSHEAR M. BRYAN JR.
Class of 1954

While assigned to the 23rd Artillery Group as a Forward Artillery Controller (FAC), John disappeared on August 8, 1966 while flying cover in his L-19 Bird Dog for a vehicle convoy along Highway One between Ben Hoa and Xaun Loc. Seven months later, ground forces found the crash site and recovered John's remains from the shot-up aircraft.

Having branched to the Air Force upon graduation, Captain Blackshear requested reassignment to the Army in 1964. On Sept 27, 1967 in Vung Tau province, he was killed in a crash during a U-21A training mission while avoiding trespassers on the runway. Major Blackshear is buried next to his father, Lt. General Blackshear M. Bryan, USMA '23, 43rd Superintendent of West Point, and his brother Jamie USMA '65, who died in an military air accident near Kirkland NM in 1977.

PETER J. LANTZ
Class of 1966

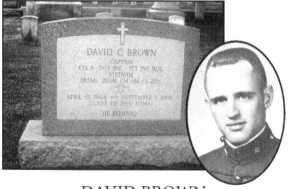

DAVID BROWN
Class of 1966

Serving as a platoon leader with the 2nd Battalion, 503rd Infantry Regiment, Lantz was another casualty of the week-long fight to take Hill 875. Lantz died in an assault on heavily fortified NVA positions on November 23, 1967.

As a company commander in the 503rd Infantry, 173rd Airborne Brigade, he was killed in action in the Quang Duc Province on September 17, 1968.

IRAQ: OPERATIONS DESERT SHIELD/ STORM

The complex politics of oil, national rivalries, and militaristic regimes in the Middle East boiled over once more in August of 1990 when Iraq invaded and seized its oil-rich neighbor Kuwait. This posed an unacceptable threat to world oil supplies and other states in the region. President George H.W. Bush led an international coalition to first prevent further advances of Saddam Hussein's troops, and then liberate Kuwait. The coalition led by General H. Norman Schwarzkopf scrambled to establish a defensive shield around Saudi Arabia with 530,000 U.S. troops and 120,000 from coalition members.

Once the perimeter was established, plans were developed for an assault on Iraq's position. The Storm began on January 17, 1990 with a six- week aerial bombardment campaign to cripple Iraq's military ability to function effectively. On February 24, 1991 coalition forces invaded Iraq and Kuwait to destroy Iraqi forces. The Iraqis were overwhelmed in a ground war that lasted just 100 hours. The operation was characterized by a huge end run around the Iraqi forces by the US Army's VII Corps and the XVII Airborne Corps. The Iraqis were surrounded and quickly surrendered.

America had 145 soldiers killed in action, including one West Pointer - Lieutenant Donaldson Tillar '88 who died when the Blackhawk helicopter in which he was riding was shot down.

H. NORMAN SCHWARZKOPF Jr.
1934-2012
Class of 1956

Norman Schwarzkopf Jr. was born in Trenton, New Jersey, the son of a West Point graduate and later Major General who is also buried at West Point. Schwarzkopf was raised in both the United States and Iran, graduating from West Point in 1956. He served in the Viet Nam War, first as an adviser to the South Vietnamese Army and later as a battalion commander. He was awarded three Silver Star Medals, two Purple Hearts, and the Legion of Merit.

Schwarzkopf rose quickly through the officer corps to command the U.S. 24th Infantry Division and was one of the commanders of Operation Urgent Fury, the invasion of Grenada in 1983. Building his reputation as a hard-driving military commander with a temper, he was also noted for his abilities as a military diplomat and in dealing with the press. In 1988 Schwarzkopf was tapped to run the US Central Command-CENTCOM- which includes countries in the Middle East, North Africa, and Central Asia, and most notably Afghanistan and Iraq.

As the CENTCOM commander, Schwarzkopf was called upon to respond to the Iraq invasion of Kuwait in 1990. His command expanded to an international force of over 750,000 troops. After diplomatic relations broke down, he planned and led Operation Desert Storm—an extended air campaign followed by a highly successful 100-hour ground offensive—which destroyed the Iraqi Army and liberated Kuwait in early 1991. Schwarzkopf became a national hero after organizing and leading one of the most successful campaigns in U.S. military history.

Schwarzkopf retired shortly after the end of the war and undertook a number of philanthropic ventures, rarely venturing into the political spotlight. He died in late 2012 from complications of pneumonia.

IRAQ: OPERATION IRAQI FREEDOM

The Iraq War, or Operation Iraqi Freedom, arose from the United States' conviction that Iraqi President Saddam Hussein possessed weapons of mass destruction (WMD) - nuclear, chemical and biological - and posed a threat to the region's security. In 2002, the United Nations Security Council passed a resolution calling for Iraq to cooperate with UN weapon inspectors in verifying that Iraq was not in possession of WMD and cruise missiles. The United Nations monitoring commission, hampered by the Iraqi government, could not verify Iraq's assurances regarding possession of WMD.

The United States and its allies invaded Iraq in March 2003, which led to an occupation and the capture of President Saddam Hussein. He was later tried in an Iraqi court of law and executed for crimes against the Iraqi people. Violence against coalition forces and among sectarian groups evolved into the Iraqi insurgency, deadly strife between Sunni and Shia Iraqi groups. U.S. efforts were focused on rebuilding the country and establishing an enduring representative government to govern Iraq.

By 2006 international public opinion shifted in favor of reducing the presence of troops enabling Iraqi forces to begin taking responsibility for security. The UN members started their forces withdrawal. In 2008 the U.S. and Iraqi governments reached an agreement approving the stationing of U.S. forces only through 2011. The United States began reducing its footprint in Iraq by 2010 and removed all forces by December 2011. The sectarian violence continues, however, with thousands of Iraqi casualties each year.

The U.S. suffered 4,805 combat deaths in Iraq, including 47 West Pointers. Thirteen other West Pointers died in non-combat related events.

At West Point, A Quiet Place to Honor Warriors
by Rick Hampson

Americans will argue for years over what was won in Iraq. To understand what was lost, come to the U.S. Military Academy cemetery and walk through Section 36, a garden of unrealized potential and thwarted dreams that sits on a windy bluff over the Hudson River.

Separated only by a hedge from a parking lot, Section 36 is the newest and least picturesque part of a cramped old graveyard that lacks the sweeping, aching grandeur of Arlington or the American cemetery at Normandy.

But there is loss and ache here enough.

See the big polished granite stone of Emily Perez, the highest-ranking minority female cadet in West Point history. On Sept. 12, 2006, she became the first female academy graduate and the first member of the Class of 2005, to die in Iraq.....

Walk a few feet and stop at the simple white military-issue marker of Col. Theodore Westhusing. It says he died June 5, 2005. It doesn't say that he was a philosophy doctorate-holder who at age 44 left a wife, three kids and a teaching job at West Point to volunteer for Iraq; that he said the experience would make him a better teacher; that he shot himself a month before he was due home, becoming at the time the highest-ranking soldier to die in Iraq.

Move on to the graves of Captains Stephen Frank and Jay Harting, Michigan boys who graduated from West Point together, went to Iraq together and died together while inspecting a suicide bomber's car trunk. That was April 29, 2005, two weeks before Harting was due home for the birth of his son.

A few steps away, in Row E, lies Lt. Michael Adams. On March 16, 2004, he was in a convoy headed out of Iraq and toward home when he was killed in a collision with a U.S. contractor's vehicle. The barrel of his tank swung around on impact, hitting him in the head. He was 24. "Next time you hear from me," he had e-mailed his parents a few days earlier, "it will be from Kuwait."

A cemetery at war's end is as much about what never will be as what was. Bill Hecker, '91, will never come back to West Point to teach Poe and Twain. Eric Paliwoda, '97, will never throw another tailgate party at Michie Stadium. Tom Martin, '05, will never make general. Matthew August, '97, will never catch another trout or bag another deer. His classmate, Mike MacKinnon, will never have another burger at the York Bar in his native Helena, Mont.

Nineteen 'young treasures'

The cemetery harbors the remains of 19 of the 59 West Point graduates who died in Iraq. They're among the 4,474 U.S. military personnel killed in that conflict. Although the Iraq war is over, the one in Afghanistan may provide Section 36 with more headstones.......

Former cadets have accounted for a higher proportion of the dead in Iraq and Afghanistan than in any other recent war, partly because of the ubiquity of hidden bombs, partly because of the peril to junior officers leading patrols and partly because academy graduating classes are larger. In Iraq about 1.3% of the U.S. dead were former cadets, three times higher than in Viet Nam or Korea and six times higher than in World War II.

The 19 buried here include nine lieutenants, eight captains, one major and one colonel. All but four had yet to turn 30. Only one was over 40. They left 17 children (none older than 12), 11 widows, and four fiancées or steady girlfriends. One of the wives and two of the fiancées were themselves serving in Iraq when their men fell there.

More than half of the 19, including Emily Perez, died in roadside bombings, never seeing what or who hit them. Lt. Andy Houghton was hit by a rocket-propelled grenade while on patrol; he lingered for a month at Walter Reed hospital with shrapnel wounds before succumbing, shortly after receiving his Purple Heart.

Most had a family connection to the military. Many were Army brats, children of colonels and sergeants who grew up on posts around the world. They played with GI Joe and wore fatigues at Halloween; Phil Neel, buried next to Houghton over by the river, drafted ants and doodlebugs to participate in war games.

The residents of Section 36 first came to West Point as valedictorians, varsity captains, Eagle Scouts, youth group leaders, JROTC commanders. "These were young treasures that we lost," says Conrad Crane, '74, director of the Army Military History Institute. This is where West Point's ideal of service meets its ideal of sacrifice, and the Long Gray Line finally ends. It's where the traditions of Graduation Week — the weddings, the final procession on the parade field, the hats flung in the air after commencement — are replaced by the folded flag, the three-volley salute, and Taps.

It's a reversal of fortune as stark as any in American life. "This place," says Col. Thomas Kolditz, who parachuted with Neel and still can hear Perez' booming laugh out in the hall, "is a great equalizer...."

JAMES FRANCIS ADAMOUSKI
1973–2003
Class of 1995

Piloting a Black Hawk helicopter Adamouski crashed on April 2, 2003, the first West Pointer to die in Iraq. He is buried at Arlington National Cemetery, but has a memorial here at West Point.

DENNIS L. PINTOR
1974–2004
Class of 1998

Captain Dennis L. Pintor of Killeen, Texas, died in Baghdad, Iraq, on 12 October 2004 when an improvised explosive detonated near his vehicle.

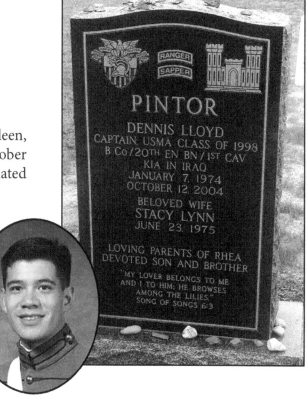

DAVID R. BERNSTEIN
1979-2003
Class of 2001

First Lieutenant Bernstein was on a patrol convoy on October 18, 2003 when insurgents opened fire with rocket-propelled grenades, killing one soldier in his unarmored Humvee. The wounded driver drove into a field and fell out the door trapping his arm beneath the vehicle. Bernstein, though suffering a severe leg wound, endeavored several times to pull himself into the driver's seat. The fifth time he succeeded and rolled the Humvee off the driver's arm. The bullet had severed Dave's femoral artery. When help arrived, Bernstein was dead. He was awarded the Silver Star.

NEALE M. SHANK
1981-2007
Class of 2005

First Lieutenant Shank served with the 10th Mountain Division from Fort Drum, N.Y. He enlisted after graduation from high school in 1999, then was accepted into the U.S. Military Academy at West Point, graduating in 2005. Shank died on March 31, 2007 in Baghdad from a non-combat-related incident.

JONATHAN W. EDDS
1983-2007
Class of 2005

First Lieutenant Edds died in Baghdad, Iraq, of wounds suffered when insurgents attacked his vehicle using an improvised explosive device and small arms fire. He was serving with the 69th Armor Regiment, 3rd Infantry Division, Fort Benning, Ga.

GARRISON C. AVERY
1982-2006
Class of 2004

First Lieutenant Avery died in Baghdad, Iraq, when an improvised explosive device detonated near his HMMWV. He was serving with 502nd Infantry Regiment, 101st Airborne Division, Fort Campbell, KY.

DENNIS W. ZILINSKI II
1981-2005
Class of 2004

First Lieutenant Zilinski II was a rifle platoon leader with the 3rd Brigade Combat Team (Rakkasans), 101st Airborne Division out of Fort Campbell, Kentucky. He and three other soldiers were killed when an improvised explosive device detonated near their HMMWV during combat operations in Bayji, Iraq.

AFGHANISTAN

Responding to the September 11, 2001 attacks on the United States, the forces of the United States, United Kingdom, Australia, and the Afghan Northern Alliance launched Operation Enduring Freedom on October 2001. The dual objectives were to destroy the al-Qaeda terrorist organization and prevent the use of Afghanistan as a terrorist base. To this end the United States intended to remove the Taliban regime from ruling Afghanistan and establish representative government. Eleven years later the U.S. continues the struggle against a widespread Taliban insurgency. Moreover the war has expanded into the mountains of neighboring Pakistan. This is the United States' longest running war.

Though mid-2013, the United States has suffered over 2,264 deaths including 34 West Pointers.

MICHAEL J. McMAHON
1963-2004
Class of 1985

In November 2004 Lieutenant Colonel McMahon died in a plane crash high in the snow-capped mountains of Afghanistan becoming the highest ranking Army officer killed in that country during Operation Enduring Freedom.

THOMAS E. KENNEDY
1977-2012
Class of 2000

Having already served two tours in Iraq, Major Kennedy was killed in August 2012 along with a command sgt major, an Air Force major, and a civilian when a bomber detonated a suicide vest in Sarkowi, Afghanistan. He was serving with the Headquarters Company, 4th Brigade Combat Team, 4th Infantry Division, Fort Carson, CO.

LAURA M. WALKER,
1977-2005
Class of 2003

First Lieutenant Walker died on August 18, 2005, in Kandahar, Afghanistan, when an improvised explosive device detonated underneath her HMMWV during ground assault convoy operations. She was the first female graduate of West Point to be killed in combat. Lieutenant Walker was the granddaughter, daughter, and sister of West Pointers.

TIMOTHY J. STEELE
1985-2011
Class of 2009

First Lieutenant Steele died in Kandahar province, Afghanistan, of wounds suffered when insurgents attacked his unit using an improvised explosive device. He was assigned to the 87th Infantry Regiment 10th Mountain Division, Fort Drum, N.Y.

93

MATHEW FERRARA
1983-2007
Class of 2005

JAIMIE LEONARD
1974 - 2013
Class of 1997

Lt. Ferrara, serving with the 2nd Battalion, 503rd Airborne Infantry Regiment, died of wounds sustained when his patrol was attacked by enemy forces in Aranus, Afghanistan, on Nov 9, 2007. Six other soldiers also died in the ambush following a meeting with elders at a nearby village.

Major Leonard was on her second tour in Afghanistan with the 10th Mountain Division. She was one of three New Yorkers killed on June 8, 2013 when the Afghan soldier they were training turned his weapon on them and killed her, a fellow officer, and a civilian contractor. She was posthumously promoted to lieutenant colonel.

Temporary marker

94

FACULTY, STAFF & AUTHORS

LOUIS BENTZ
1808-1878
Not a Graduate

Old Bentz served as the Academy's bugler for 32 years. He and his dog were constant sights around the post, and were fondly regarded by the cadets.

SUSAN and ANNA WARNER
Not Graduates

Known as the Bronte Sisters of America, they wrote seven children's books, and taught Bible classes to the cadets for over sixty years. Susan wrote *The Wide, Wide World* in 1850 which became a best seller of its day. Anna is best known for writing the words to the hymn *Jesus Loves Me*. They lived on Constitution Island, which is a few hundred yards by boat from Trophy Point. Anna was given a full military funeral with the entire corps of cadets as her escort. Dwight D. Eisenhower had been one of her pupils. Their home and the island itself are part of the Academy and maintained for visitors by the Constitution Island Association.

DENNIS HART MAHAN
1802–1871
Not a Graduate

Dennis Hart Mahan, professor at West Point West Point from 1824 to 1871. Mahan single-handedly compiled and transferred the principles of European engineering to the United States. Most 19th century engineering schools in the United States were started with West Point-educated faculty or its textbooks. The Civil War commanders, whether Union or Confederate, learned about entrenchment, fortifications, and how to conduct warfare in his classes at West Point, and from his writings. He is the father of eminent naval historian and theorist Rear Admiral Alfred Thayer Mahan, author of the *Influence of Sea Power Upon History,* 1660 - 1873.

WILLIAM SAUNDERS
1835-1906
Not a graduate

According to his memorial, Saunders served the Academy for a half century in the vital roles of hospital steward, dental surgeon, and undertaker.

JEANNE HUTCHISON
1966 -2009
Class of 1988

Academics, physical, and military are the key components of the cadet education. Central to their military development are the Tactical Officers under the Commandant of Cadets. "Tacs" are active duty officers who return to West Pont to impart their knowledge of military practices and leadership to the future officers. Lieutenant Colonel Hutchison had completed her battalion command at the 551st Signal Corps Unit in Fort Gordon GA and was the Tactical Officer in charge of the Second Regiment of the Corps Cadets upon her untimely death from natural causes.

MARTY MAHER
1876–1961
Not a Graduate

Martin Maher was an Irish immigrant who joined the United States Army in 1898 rising to the rank of master sergeant. He served over 50 years at West Point. He was a swimming instructor from 1899 to 1928. Maher retired from the Army in 1928 and stayed at West Point as a civilian employee. He retired from that in 1946, beloved by the many classes he coached and served. His autobiography, *Bringing Up The Brass: My 55 Years at West Point*, published in 1951, was the basis for the film *The Long Gray Line* featuring Tyrone Power as Maher and Maureen O'Hara as his wife.

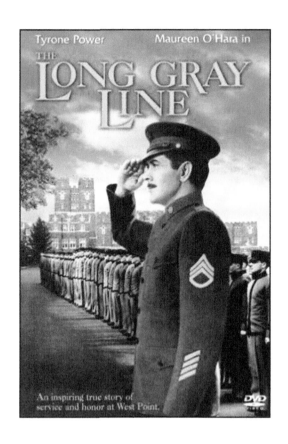

RUSSELL REEDER Jr.
1902–1998
Class of 1926

Russell Potter Reeder Jr. was a soldier, athlete, and notable author of fiction and non-fiction about America's wars and West Point. His memoir "Born at Reveille" (as the saluting gun boomed at Fort Leavenworth, Kansas, in 1902) describes his youth as an Army brat. An excellent athlete, "Red" Reeder graduated from West Point in 1926. He returned to West Point from 1929 to 1936 as an assistant coach of the Army football team,

He served in the Southwest Pacific in 1942 preparing a report entitled "Fighting on Guadalcanal" which General Marshall distributed to all troops in training for combat. Moving to Europe in 1944, he commanded the 12th Infantry Regiment of the 4th Infantry Division, the third regiment ashore on Utah Beach which made the greatest advance at the end of the first day. "Red" Reeder gave new meaning to the phrase, "leading by example" as he moved at the forefront of his command. He was awarded the Distinguished Service Cross, the first such award made in France. On June 11, a German artillery round badly wounded him, causing the loss of his left leg.

Reeder retired from the Army in 1945, but was asked by Superintendent Maxwell Taylor to establish a course in leadership. He also coached the Army baseball teams. His "final" retirement from the Army was in 1967 to continue his writing career. He authored a popular series of six books for youth featuring a fictional Clint Lane as he journeyed from plebe to first classman and then to service as a junior officer in Berlin and Korea.

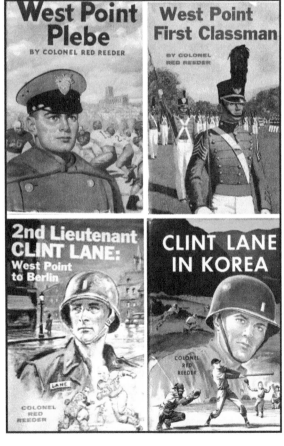

ARMY SPORTS & SPIRIT

PAUL BUNKER
1881–1943
Class of 1903

GARRISON HOLT DAVIDSON
1904–1992
Class of 1927

Bunker is a football immortal, an All-American in both 1901 and 1902. In the Philippines during WW II but before his lines were overrun by the Japanese, he and his men lowered and buried the American flag to prevent its capture. He smuggled it past his captors and preserved it until his death in the P.O.W. camp. The remnants of that flag now reside in the West Point museum.

"Gar" was a successful pre-war football coach at the Academy and rival of Red Blaik, as well as a distinguished leader in both World War II and Korea. Davidson served as Superintendent from 1956 to 1960 and altered the cadet curriculum by introducing electives. Cadets no longer needed to follow exactly the same program.

EARL "RED" BLAIK
1897-1989
Class of 1920

Red Blaik was head football coach from 1941 to 1958. His years were noted for an intense rivalry with Frank Leahy of Notre Dame with each team seeming to battle each other for the national championship year after year. Blaik's team won the national title in three consecutive years 1944-1946.

GLENN W. DAVIS
1924–2005
Class of 1947

Davis was one of Army's most famous football players. A three-time All-America, he led Army to national titles in 1944-45. Known as "Mr Outside," he formed half of a famous rushing duo with Doc Blanchard, known as "Mr. Inside." Glenn Davis won the Heisman Trophy in 1946. After completing his military service, he played professional football for the Los Angeles Rams before a knee injury ended his career.

PHILIP EGNER
1880-1956
Not a Graduate

Phillip Egner, an accomplished cellist and member of the NY Metropolitan Orchestra, assumed the position as 1st Lieutenant and West Point's Teacher of Music in May 1917. He brought exceptional musical talent to his position at West Point, producing many football fight songs, most notably "On Brave Old Army Team." He also produced the "Official West Point March," and wrote or arranged all the music for each 100th Night Show for over 20 years.

MAGGIE DIXON
1977–2006
Not a Graduate

Maggie Dixon was born in California and played basketball at the University of San Diego. After an unsuccessful try out for the WNBA she became an assistant coach at DePaul University in 2001.

In 2005, just 11 days before the 2005-2006 season, Dixon was hired as the women's basketball coach of the United States Military Academy. In her first year the team won 20 games while losing 11 and winning the Patriot League conference tournament. The team went to the 2006 NCAA Women's Division I Basketball Tournament as a 15th seed, but lost to the University of Tennessee. It was the first March Madness tournament appearance for any Army basketball team.

Shortly after her only season at West Point, Maggie Dixon died suddenly of heart disease.

RONALD ZINN
1939–1965
Class of 1962

Ron Zinn represented the United States at the Olympics in 1960 and 1964 as a race walker. He died in a firefight near Saigon while serving with the 173rd Airborne Brigade.

GEORGE W. GOETHALS
1858-1928
Class of 1880

Because of his leadership in completing the Panama Canal, George Washington Goethals will always be remembered as one of the builders of what has been called "America's Empire." At West Point he was president of his class and rose to the rank of cadet captain before graduating second in his class of 523 cadets. He served with the Engineers athroughout the United States for 27 years, but the opportunity for fame came in 1907.

For 30 years the French, under de Lesseps, who had built the Suez Canal, were attempting to build a canal across Panama. After struggling with disease, terrain, financial mismanagement, and poor organization, the French finally gave up, stating the job was impossible.

The United States then stepped up to the task. In late 1907 President Teddy Roosevelt appointed Goethals to lead the effort giving him total control of all activities at or near the proposed canal.

Goethals set about establishing what amounted to a small country with its own judicial system, post office and police along with schools, storehouses, hotels, kitchens, machine shops, and even a railroad. Especially important was a medical department under William C. Gorgas, charged with eliminating the problem of yellow fever. There were, of course, immense engineering problems with no comparable experiences to serve as guides.

When the canal was completed in 1914, Goethals became a hero to the world, receiving decorations from many countries. He retired from active duty in 1917, but was recalled to duty that same year as acting quartermaster general when World War I broke out for the United States. He became responsible for the movement of all troops and supplies to Europe. In 1919 he again left the army and set up his own construction company which prospered with many projects around the country. Failing health forced his retirement in 1927, and he died of cancer on January 21, 1928.

YING-HSING WEN
1887-1968
Class of 1909

With the permission of Congress, Wen became the first Chinese cadet at West Point. Intelligent and amiable, he soon established his popularity in the Corps of Cadets. Upon graduation, he returned to China as a military aide to Dr. Sun Yat-Sen working to overthrow the Manchu dynasty. He rose through the officer corps of the Nationalist Army to serve as a deputy commanding general under Chiang Kai-Shek. With the Communist triumph in mainland China, Wen fled with the Nationalist forces to Taiwan. He eventually moved to America.

H. NORMAN SCHWARZKOPF SR.
1895-1958
Class of 1917

Upon graduation from West Point, H. Norman Schwarzhopf Sr. joined the American Expeditionary Force in France and suffered a disabling mustard gas attack. He later served as a provost marshal of a military police command in Germany following the war.

Returning to the United States as a Colonel, Schwarzkopf resigned to accept an appointment as head of the New Jersey State Police, organizing it from its inception. He achieved national recognition while heading that agency during the investigation of the Lindbergh kidnapping case.

With the onset of World War II, Schwarzkopf re-enlisted in the Army and was posted to Iran, tasked with organizing the Iranian police after the UK-Soviet intervention that made Iran an Allied protectorate. Following the war, he was promoted to brigadier general and served in Germany as provost marshal for the U.S. sector.

Schwarzkopf returned to Iran in the early fifties at the behest of the Central Intelligence Agency to persuade the self-exiled Iranian monarch, Mohammad Reza Shah, to return and seize power, which he did. He retired in 1953 with the rank of major general.

Norman Schwarzkopf Sr. is the father of Norman Schwarzkopf Jr. who commanded coalition forces to a great victory in the first Iraqi War.

THE SELFRIDGE MEMORIAL

Thomas E. Selfridge, Class of 1906, was among the first Army aviators. and the first person to die in a crash of a powered airplane. He was a passenger in a plane piloted by Orville Wright when the aircraft crashed at Ft Myers Virginia in September 1908. Selfridge suffered severe injuries and died several weeks later. He is buried in Arlington National Cemetery, but this cenotaph commemorates his life and contributions to Army aviation.

DAVID MARCUS
1901-1948
Class of 1924

Born in lower Manhattan, New York, David Marcus spent much of his youth in a tough street life, but he was able to enter the Academy on July 1, 1920. He resigned from the service in 1926 to pursue a career in law. In New York he made his way to the staff of the Federal District Attorney. His public career was largely devoted to gangster-busting. These activities often took on a dangerous and violent nature.

During World War II Marcus served with distinction in several staff positions and played a role at the conferences of Dumbarton Oaks and at Quebec. After the war Marcus was sent to Germany where he served under General Clay in running the military government. In 1947 Israeli officials came to the United States seeking a man who could train their irregular forces into a modern army. Israel was being threatened by many of its Arab neighbors, and most of the world doubted the ability of the greatly outnumbered nation to hold onto its newly won independence. Marcus became the choice of these officials to make an army out of virtually nothing. He left for Palestine in January, 1948, putting his full energy to the task. In May, when the Arabs attacked, he was at once made Supreme Commander of the Jerusalem Front and given the task of keeping the roads to the city open. Inspecting the lines in an open jeep, he was killed by a mine explosion just twenty-four hours before a United Nations truce went into effect.

So highly did Israel regard this West Pointer that it sent the pink granite marker that adorns his grave.

EDWARD H. WHITE II
1930-1967
Class of 1952

Upon graduation from West Point in 1952, White was commissioned as a 2nd Lieutenant in the Air Force attending flight training. He then spent several years in Germany flying fighter jets. In 1959 White was selected to attend the U.S. Air Force Test Pilot School at Edwards Air Force Base and was then assigned as a test pilot at Wright-Patterson Air Force Base.

White attained the rank of lieutenant colonel and was accepted as a NASA astronaut in 1962. He gained fame as the first American to walk in space during the Gemini Four flight on June 3, 1965. White seemed assured of a brilliant future when he was killed in a flash fire on the Apollo One Spacecraft at Cape Kennedy, Florida in January 1967 along with fellow astronauts Gus Grissom and Roger Chaffee.

CADETS

The cemetery is the final resting place of many cadets who died while attending West Point. The CADET MEMORIAL near the river side of the cemetery is testimony that illness and accident claim even the youngest and most vibrant of our youth.

This memorial, made of multi-colored stones, was erected by the cadets and officers of the Academy in memory of Cadet Vincent M. Lowe, who was killed on January 1, 1817. He had eagerly volunteered to switch places with a classmate to fire the New Year cannon. Apparently a spark still glowed inside from a previous firing, setting off an explosion and hurling Lowe away from the gun. He was carried, still breathing, by fellow cadets toward the hospital, but died before getting there. Since then, the names of cadets and professors who died while at West Point have been added to the memorial.

The Corps of Cadets observes the passing of a fellow cadet with a special private ceremony. At the noon meal, an evening vigil is announced for the departed classmate, indicating time and dress code. That evening after sunset cadets silently move from their barracks to the concrete apron in front of Washington Hall. Facing the Plain, they honor the deceased in the majesty of the sky, the mountains, and the silent Hudson River flowing before them. Not a word is spoken. When the assemblage is complete, a lone bugler plays Taps. As the last bugle note fades into the night, the cadets turn and wordlessly drift back to their barracks. Be thou at Peace.

CHARLES FRANK
Class of 1857

WARWICK M. McCRAY
Class of 1888

JAMES DARRELL GREENLEE
Class of 1969

GEORGE H. MYER
Class of 1895

REXFORD P. STORCH
Class of 1999

CONGRESSIONAL MEDAL OF HONOR RECIPIENTS BURIED AT THE WEST POINT CEMETERY

Each of these individuals is honored by small bronze plaque placed before their grave stone, and a larger brass plaque describing their heroism and selflessness. The latter are placed in and around the cadet barracks and public buildings at West Point. Several may be viewed in the main stairway area at Eisenhower "Ike" Hall.

DANIEL BUTTERFIELD
Major General
1831–1901
Not a Graduate

During the Battle of Gaines Mill, Virginia Jun 27, 1862, he took up the colors and rallied the troops while under fire. See previous biography.

WILLIAM HENRY BENYAURD
First Lieutenant
1841–1900
Class of 1863

For valor in action April 01, 1865 at Five Forks, with Engineers, US Army. With one companion, voluntarily advanced in a reconnaissance beyond the skirmishers, where he was exposed to imminent peril; also, in the same battle, rode to the front with the commanding general to encourage wavering troops to resume the advance, which they did successfully.

JOHN MOULDER WILSON
First Lieutenant
1837–1919
Class of 1860

For valor in action August 06, 1862 at Malvern Hill, VA with the US Engineers.

EUGENE ASA CARR
Colonel
1830-1910
Class of 1850

For valor in action on March 07, 1862 at Pea Ridge, AR with the 3d Illinois Cavalry, Directed the deployment of his command and held his ground, under a brisk fire of shot and shell in which he was wounded several times.

ALEXANDER STEWART WEBB
Brigadier General
1835–1911
Class of 1855

For valor in action July 03, 1863 at Gettysburg, PA with US Volunteers.

WILLIAM SULLY BEEBE
First Lieutenant
1841–1898
Class of 1863

For valor in action April 23, 1864 at Cane River Crossing, LA with the Ordinance Department, US Army. Exposed himself to great danger by voluntarily making his way through the enemy's lines to communicate with Gen. Sheridan. While rendering this service he was captured, but escaped; again came in contact with the enemy, was again ordered to surrender, but escaped by dashing away under fire.

ROBERT LEE HOWZE
Second Lieutenant
1864–1926
Class of 1888

For valor in action January 01, 1891 at White River, SD with Company K, 6th U.S. Cavalry.

GEORGE LEWIS GILLESPIE JR.
First Lieutenant
1841-1913
Class of 1862

For valor in action May 31, 1864 at Bethesda Church, VA with the Engineer Corps, US Army.

JOHN WILKINSON HEARD
First Lieutenant
1860-1922
Class of 1883

For valor in action July 23, 1898 at Bahia Honda, Cuba with 3d US Cavalry. After 2 men had been shot down by Spaniards while transmitting orders to the engine-room on the Wanderer, the ship having become disabled, Lieutenant Heard took the position held by them and personally transmitted the orders, remaining at his post until the ship was out of danger.

115

JOSEPH A. SLADEN
Private
1841 - 1911
Not a Graduate

At the Battle of Resaca, Georgia in May 14, 1864. While detailed as clerk at headquarters, voluntarily engaged in action at a critical moment of the battle. His personal example inspired the troops to repel the enemy. He was offered a commission and rose to the rank of Major in the Union Army. He later graduated from medical school and fought in the Indian Wars. Sladen accompanied Gen. Oliver Howard on a successful attempt to make peace with the Apache leader who fought a lengthty battle against the U.S. government and settlements in Apache territory. His field notes were later published as *Making Peace with Cochise,* which is still in print.

ALBERT LEOPOLD MILLS
Captain, Asst. Adj. Gen
1854-1916
Class of 1879

For valor in action July 01, 1898 at Santiago, Cuba with US Volunteers. Distinguished gallantry in encouraging those near him by his bravery and coolness after being shot through the head and entirely without sight.

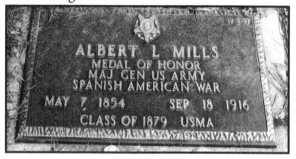

MOSES HARRIS
Major
1839 - 1927
Not a Graduate

For valor in action on August 28, 1864 at Smithfield VA leading an attack on Confederate forces resulting in an enemy rout.

WILLIAM HALE WILBUR
Colonel
1888–1979
Class of 1912

SAMUEL STREIT COURSEN
First Lieutenant
1926 –1950
Class of 1949

For valor in action November 08, 1942, at Fedala, North Africa with Western Task Force, North Africa. Wilbur led an attack against a French artillery battery. One of the few French guns still firing in the area, the battery was targeting Allied ships off shore. Wilbur gathered four tanks and a company of infantry to assault the position. He personally accompanied the group, riding along on the lead tank, and commanded them in the successful capture of the battery.

For valor in action: October 12, 1950 - Kaesong, Korea with Company C, 5th Cavalry Regiment, 1st Cavalry Division. In the battle for Hill 174, Coursen observed that one of the men of his platoon had entered a well-hidden gun emplacement, thought to be unoccupied, and had taken a bullet. Coursen ran to his aid and without regard for his personal safety, engaged the enemy in hand-to-hand combat to protect the wounded soldier until he himself was killed. When his body was recovered after the battle, seven enemy dead were found in the emplacement. Coursen's actions saved the wounded soldier's life and eliminated the main position of the enemy roadblock.

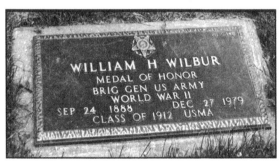

ANDRE CAVARO LUCAS
Lieutenant Colonel
1930–1970
Class of 1954

For valor in action July 01 - 23, 1970 - FSB Ripcord, Viet Nam with 2d Battalion, 506th Infantry, 101st Airborne Division. The fire base was cotinually subject to heavy attacks by a numerically superior enemy force. Lt. Col. Lucas, forsaking his own safety, performed numerous acts of extraordinary valor in directing the defense of the allied position. On one occasion, he flew in a helicopter at treetop level above an entrenched enemy directing the fire of one of his companies for over three hours. Even though his helicopter was heavily damaged by enemy fire, he remained in an exposed position until the company expended its supply of grenades. He then transferred to another helicopter, dropped critically needed grenades to the troops, and resumed his perilous mission of directing fire on the enemy. These courageous actions by Lt. Col. Lucas prevented the company from being encircled and destroyed by a larger enemy force. On another occasion, Lt. Col. Lucas attempted to rescue a crewman trapped in a burning helicopter. As the flames in the aircraft spread, and enemy fire became intense, Lt. Col. Lucas ordered all members of the rescue party to safety. Then, at great personal risk, he continued the rescue effort amid concentrated enemy mortar fire. Lt. Col. Lucas was mortally wounded while directing the successful withdrawal of his battalion from the fire base. His actions throughout this extended period inspired his men to heroic efforts, and were instrumental in saving the lives of many of his fellow soldiers while inflicting heavy casualties on the enemy.

SUPERINTENDENTS BURIED AT WEST POINT

Many of the roads at West Point are named after Superintendents.
Each has a portrait hanging in the mess hall.

SYLVANUS THAYER
See previous biography.

RENE E. DeRUSSY
Class of 1812

Term as Superintendent 1833-1838. Inventor of the Barbette depressing gun cartridge. Had four wives. Has distinction of being only goat of any class to later become Superintendent.

WESLEY MERRITT
See previous biography.

JOHN M. WILSON
Class of 1860

Term as Superintendent 1889-1893. Only member of his class to graduate with no demerits for his entire first year; an achievement he never forgot. See previous biography under Medal of Honor Recipients.

ALBERT L. MILLS
Class of 1879

Term as Superintendent 1898-1906. Only Thayer had a longer term as head of the Academy. He banned hazing at the school, and started a policy of allowing the faculty a year leave of absence so as to better their knowledge by advanced study in their fields. See previous biography under Medal of Honor Recipients.

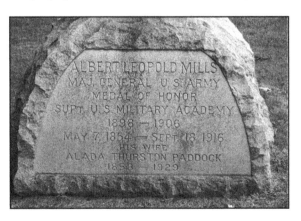

119

THOMAS H. BARRY
Class of 1877

Term as Superintendent 1910-1912. Served in every grade from cadet to major general. Thomas was a strict disciplinarian who loved West Point, and was a friend to every cadet, especially those having troubles with their studies.

JOHN BIDDLE
Class of 1881

Term as Superintendent 1916 - 1917. Graduated second in his class. Was a professor of Practical Military Engineering.

CLARENCE PACE TOWNSLEY
Class of 1881

Term as Superintendent 1912-1916. During his time the enrollment went from 700 to 1,300. His term saw the construction of a new mess hall, South wing of the South Barracks, a new barracks and an addition to the hospital. He recommended that cadet appointments be made by competitive examinations.

SAMUEL E. TILLMAN
Class of 1869

Term as Superintendent 1917-1919. Had been a full professor of history at the age of 33 and continued teaching for 31 years. Started the grading system that is still in effect. After retiring he returned to the teaching staff during WW I to free a younger man for active duty.

FRED W. SLADEN
Class of 1890

Term as Superintendent 1922-1926. An Army brat who grew up at the Academy where his father served as Adjutant. Always considered West Point his home.

MERCH B. STEWART
Class of 1896

Term as Superintendent 1926- 1927. Commandant of Cadets 1923-1926. Entered West Point when he was only 17; nicknamed Babe. He did much to modernize arrangements that that had been in effect for decades.

EDWIN B. WINANS
Class of 1891

Term as Superintendent 1928. He gained his commission into the Cavalry and went on to serve in the Philippines as well as in the Punitive Expedition to Mexico in 1916. During World War I he commanded the 64th Infantry Brigade, 32nd Division of the American Expeditionary Force. After the war, Winans took command of the 10th Cavalry at Fort Huachuca, Arizona before becoming Superintendent.

WILLIAM R. SMITH
Class of 1892

Term of Superintendent from 1928-1932. Attended Vanderbilt University before his appointment to West Point graduating 10th out of 62 cadets in his class. He served in the Field Artillery and as an instructor at West Point teaching scientific and military subjects.   Prior to World War I, Smith served in Coast Artillery and supervised the first anti-submarine net laid down by the United States, extending from Fort Monroe to Fort Wool to close the entrance to Hampton Roads. He commanded the 36th Infantry Division in France at the end of the war.

GARRISON HOLT DAVIDSON
Class of 1927

Term as Superintendent 1956-1960. See previous biography in Army Sports and Spirit.

BRYANT E. MOORE
Class of 1917

Term as Superintendent 1949-1951. See previous biography under Korean War.

WILLIAM D. CONNOR
Class of 1897

Term as Superintendent 1932–1938. Graduated #1 in his class. As Superintendent, he negotiated an understanding with the Naval Academy in 1932 on the eligibility of players for football. Army was allowing players with three years prior college experience to play for the Black Knights, while Navy followed the intercollegiate three year rule and wouldn't play them. They agreed to disagree for three more years, although Navy and the NCAA eventually prevailed.

Connor was also the recipient in 1937 of a famous, widely-publicized letter from General Simon Bolivar Buckner, Jr. (USMA '08) on the preparation of mint juleps. It went to great length about gathering, preparing, and mixing the ingredients before concluding:

"Thus harmoniously blended by the deft touches of a skilled hand, you have a beverage eminently appropriate for honorable men and beautiful women. When all is ready, assemble your guests on the porch or in the garden where the aroma of the juleps will rise heavenward and make the birds sing. Propose a worthy toast, raise the goblets to your lips, bury your nose in the mint, inhale a deep breath of its fragrance and sip the nectar of the gods. Being overcome with thirst, I can write no further."

FRANCIS WILBY
Class of 1905

Term as Superintendent 1942-1945. Developed a three-year curriculum in order to graduate cadets more rapidly for service in WWII.

FREDERICK AUGUSTUS IRVING
Class of 1917

Participated in the St. Mihiel offensive with World War I and commended the 24th Division in the Southwest Pacific in World War II. Term as Superintendent 1951-1954. He served the Army for 37 years retiring in 1954. At the time of his death at 101 years in 1995 he was the oldest living graduate.

123

BLACKSHEAR M. BRYAN
Class of 1922

Branched to artillery upon graduation, but spent most of the years before World War II in staff positions and as an instructor/coach at West Point. During World War II he served in the Provost Marshall's office overseeing the Japanese internment and prisoner of war camps. He served as Chief of Staff to General Mathew Ridgway after the war and was given his first combat command of the 24th Division in Korea in March 1951. He was appointed the 43rd Superintendent of West Point in 1954, serving until 1956. He retired from the Army in 1960. Two of his sons attended West Point. Both were killed in military aircraft accidents and are buried beside him.

JAMES B. LAMPERT
Class of 1936

Term as Superintendent 1963-1966 Saw expansion of enrollment from 2,500 to 4,000 and the largest building program in history. During WWII he had worked on the Manhattan Project to develop the Atomic Bomb. He also served in Viet Nam.

HOWARD D. GRAVES
Class of 1961

Term as Superintendent 1991–1996. A scholar and distinguished advisor to the Joint Chiefs and the Office of the Secretary of Defense, he commanded the United States Army War College between 1989-1991. After retiring from the Army, he was a visiting professor at the University of Texas and chancellor of The Texas A&M University System.

WILLIAM WESTMORELAND
Class of 1936

Term as Superintendent 1960-1963. See previous biography under Viet Nam.

DONALD V. BENNETT
Class of 1940

SAMUEL WILLIAM KOSTER
Class of 1942

Term as Superintendent 1966-1968. An Ohio native, he attended Michigan State Univ. before graduating from West Point. As a Lieutenant Colonel, Bennett landed with the second wave at 0720 on D-Day. He was instrumental in leading the 62nd Armored Field Artillery Battalion up from Omaha Beach. He retired in 1974 as commanding general of the U.S. Army Pacific Command.

Term Superintendent 1969-1970, Koster served in Europe during World War II, and directed guerrilla warfare operations during the Korean War. By 1967, he attained the rank of Major General in command of the Americal Division in Viet Nam. Because of his involvement in the cover up of the My Lai massacre, Koster was denied promotion to the rank of lieutenant general. He finished his career as a brigadier general at Aberdeen Proving Grounds in Maryland.

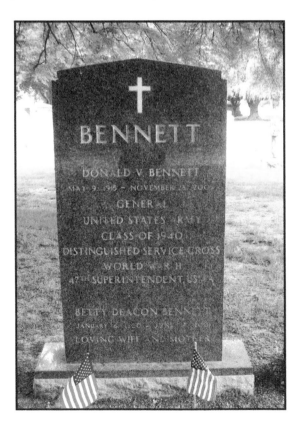

WILLARD W. SCOTT
Class of 1948

Term as Superintendent 1981-1986. Branched to field artillery upon graduation. During the Vietnam War, Scott led the 23rd Artillery Group, later commanded the 25th Infantry Division, and subsequently V Corp in Germany. He was such a devoted fan of Army football, even appearing on a mule at the Army-Navy game, that one of the mule mascots was named Scotty.

FAMILY

While there are many graves to linger over and consider, those of family members lying together provide a unique perspective--always poignant, but at times whimsical.

WHITFIELD
Robert, Class of 1948, wife Jerol, and son Richard, Class of 1971

DAVIDSON
Garrison, Class of 1927, and wife Verone

WHITE
Edward H., Class of 1924 and Family. Nearby lies their other son Edward H. White II,
the first American to walk in space. See previous biography.

TERRY
Frederick Jr, Class of 1960 killed in Viet Nam on July 4, 1968
Frederick, Class of 1930, killed during the invasion of Saipan, June 1944

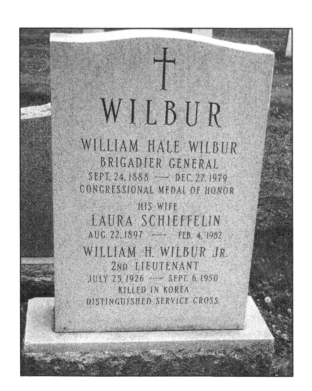

WILBUR
William H., Class of 1912, awarded Medal of Honor for heroism in North Africa, and wife Laura.   William H. Jr, Class of 1949, killed in Korea, awarded Distinguished Service Cross

FAIKS
Walter, Class of 1936, and his wife Jeanne

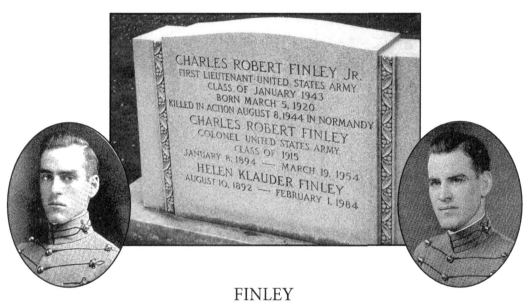

FINLEY
Charles R., Class of 1915, his wife Helen, and son Charles R. Jr. Class of 1943.

"As far back as cadet days, this dedicated West Pointer had decided that he was to be buried at West Point. On a bright sunny day in early April, he found a soldier's resting place next to that of his gallant son, "Happy" (1943), who ten years previously, as a lieutenant of the 9th Infantry, 2d Division, died in France."
From his WP-AOG memorial page.

PROMINENT WEST POINTERS WHO ARE NOT BURIED AT WEST POINT

The Registry of Graduates for 2013 lists over 70,263 graduates since 1802. There are 50,000 living grads with just over 20,000 deceased. About 6,000 thousand graduates are buried in this cemetery. Among the eminent graduates buried elsewhere:

Name	Year	Location
Joseph Sydney Johnston	1826	Austin. Texas
Jefferson Davis	1828	Richmond, Virginia
Robert E. Lee	1829	Lexington, Virginia
Joseph E. Johnston	1829	Baltimore, Maryland
George Washington Cullum	1833	Brooklyn, New York
George Gordon Meade	1835	Philadelphia, Pennsylvania
John Sedgwick	1837	Cornwall, Connecticut
Joseph Hooker	1837	Cincinnati, Ohio
Wm T. Sherman	1840	St. Louis, Missouri
Abner Doubleday	1842	Arlington National Cemetery
James E. Longstreet	1842	Gainesville, Georgia
Ulysses S. Grant	1843	New York City (Grant's Tomb!)
Winfield S. Hancock	1844	Norristown, Pennsylvania
T. "Stonewall" Jackson	1846	Lexington, Virginia
George Pickett	1846	Richmond, Virginia
George McClellan	1846	Trenton, New Jersey
John Bell Hood	1853	New Orleans, Louisiana
Ambrose P Hill	1847	Richmond, Virginia
Phillip J. Sheridan	1853	Arlington National Cemetery
John M. Schofield	1853	Arlington National Cemetery
J.E.B. Stuart	1854	Richmond, Virginia
Oliver Otis Howard	1854	Burlington, Vermont
Fitz Hugh Lee	1856	Richmond, Virginia
John J. Pershing	1886	Arlington National Cemetery
Henry Ossian Flipper	1887	Thomasville, Georgia

Peyton March	1888	Arlington National Cemetery
Douglas MacArthur	1903	Norfolk, Virginia
Jonathan Wainwright	1906	Arlington National Cemetery
Henry "Hap" Arnold	1907	Arlington National Cemetery
Simon Bolivar Buckner Jr.	1908	Frankfurt, Kentucky
George S. Patton	1909	American Cemetery, Lux.
Omar Bradley	1915	Arlington National Cemetery
Dwight Eisenhower	1915	Abilene, Kansas
Matthew Ridgway	1917	Arlington National Cemetery
Mark. W. Clark	1917	The Citadel, South Carolina
Leslie Groves	1918	Arlington National Cemetery
Lyman Lemnitzer	1920	Arlington National Cemetery
Maxwell Taylor	1922	Arlington National Cemetery
Creighton Abrams Jr.	1936	Arlington National Cemetery
Benjamin Oliver Davis Jr.	1936	Arlington National Cemetery
Felix "Doc" Blanchard	1947	San Antonio, Texas
Alexander Haig	1947	Arlington National Cemetery

George C. Marshall, Army Chief of Staff during WW II and Secretary of State under President Truman, attended Virginia Military Institute, not West Point, and is buried in Arlington National Cemetery.

WHO MAY BE BURIED IN THE CEMETERY AT WEST POINT

A graduate of the U. S. Military Academy, provided he/she also

1. Served in the U. S. Corps of Cadets as a United States citizen, was also a citizen at time of death and subsequent service in the Armed Forces of the United States, if any, terminated honorably, or

2. Served on active duty in the Armed Forces of the United States and such services terminated honorably, or

3. Served during time of war in the armed forces of a nation allied with the United States during such war, provided he/she was a United States citizen at the time of entry into such service, at time of death, and provided such military service terminated honorably.

Non-graduates who are

4. Members of the Armed Forces of the United States, including member cadets who are on active duty at the USMA at time of death.

5. Members of the Armed Forces of the United States who were on active duty at the USMA at the time of retirement or whose last duty station was USMA prior to retirement for physical disability.

6. Spouses and immediate family members of the above.

134

VISITING THE CEMETERY

Prior to September 11, 2001, the U.S. Military Academy was an "open post." Visitors could drive or walk on the post with hardly more than a salute from the soldier at the gate house This allowed thousands of people each year great freedom to stroll around and enjoy the grandeur of West Point--The Plain, the granite buildings, Trophy Point, the athletic fields, the Chapels, and the cemetery.

The Global War on Terrorism has changed that. West Point now has very restricted access. If not on official business, or escorted by a member of the U.S military, visitors may only enter the post on the following conditions:

     1. As part of an officially sanctioned tour. These are daily 90-minute and two-hour tours which may be engaged at the West Point Visitors Center outside the Thayer Gate. The two-hour tour includes the cemetery. The tours do not run on football Saturdays.

     2. On football Saturdays in the fall, civilians may walk onto the post (or drive in with a parking pass) to attend the parade of cadets and the football game. There is ample opportunity between the parade and game to stroll the quarter mile to the cemetery, browse for an hour, and hike up to Michie Stadium for the game.

     3. Civilians may also walk onto the post on certain days of great ceremony on which the Corps of Cadets is on parade--Reception Day (Monday in late June), Acceptance Day (Saturday mid-August), and Graduation Week in late May.

     4. On other days, visitors may drive on to the post through the Thayer Gate (Highland Falls) by indicating the purpose of the visit. Everyone in the vehicle must have a picture ID and the vehicle is subject to inspection.

At the caretaker's cottage there is listing of those interred and the location of their graves. There are two excellent full-color pamphlets available for the visitor:

The Trees of the West Point Cemetery - a self-guided tour
West Point Cemetery - American Heroes- Military Leaders - Army Legends

ABOUT THE SECOND EDITION

The first edition of this book, titled *Home at Rest*, was published in 1991 by Thomas E. O'Neil. Its fifty-five pages featured detailed biographies of many Civil War and WW II generals and a few other prominent graduates. Illustrated with a half-dozen black and white drawings, *Home at Rest* added rich detail to the pamphlet which visitors to the Cemetery could pick up in the Old Cadet Chapel. *Home at Rest* has been out of print for the past decade.

I observed that some eminent graduates were overlooked. Moreover, themes relating to the "less notable" and their graves deserved mention. Also, cemeteries acquire new occupants. This was certainly true as the book approached its fifteenth year since publication. In short, there was a bigger story to be told.

A few years ago I saw that the rights to *Home at Rest* were for sale on eBay. I

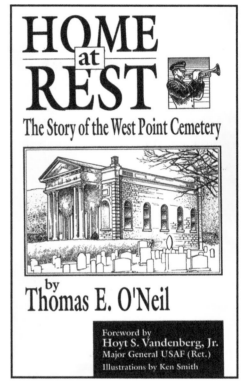

immediately bid the "Buy it Now" price and contacted Thomas O'Neil. He had retired and was looking for someone to update the book and maintain it in print, a responsibility I gladly assumed. I learned from Tom that he and his wife, Alice, spent part of their honeymoon at West Point visiting Custer's grave in the cemetery at that time, an inspiration which let to the book years later. Sadly, Mr. O'Neil passed away in April 2012.

Expanding the original *Home at Rest* was like adding several additions to a bungalow. Some significant architectural issues had to be addressed to accomplish a harmonious blend of the original with the new.

- I really couldn't continue with the in-depth biographies of the first edition, while adding a hundred more individuals, many of whom had brief careers. The imbalance was too severe. Consequently, I trimmed the lengthy biographies in the original edition to a single page or less. Custer was an exception. He was Tom O'Neil's favorite and too remarkable to 'hack away'. I left the Custer section largely untouched. If the prose seems grandiloquent, so was George Armstrong Custer.

- The biographies needed an organization. I believe that these soldiers should be seen in the context of their times. Result: I established a chapter for each of America's major wars and placed the individuals with the conflict in which they were leaders or perished. I added a synopsis of the war at the beginning of each chapter to assist the reader in recalling the history of the conflict. These summaries were inspired by the marvelous granite historical markers adjacent to each tee on the West Point Golf Course. Every hole is dedicated to one of America's conflicts. The statistics regarding deaths and Medal of Honor recipients were taken from those markers.

- I also added chapters on noteworthy graduates organizing them by Faculty, Writers, Sports and Spirit, Cadets, and Other Eminent graduates. Since many famous graduates are not buried at West Point, I added a table for those who might wonder, "Where is Douglas MacArthur or George Patton buried?"
- To enhance the biographies, I added a photograph of the individual's grave. Many were taken over Memorial Day 2010 and 2013, and thus were decorated with flowers, flags, and mementos. The graves enhanced the biographies, but failed to capture the vitality of these men and women who stepped forward in our country's defense. We decided to add a photo of each of the deceased. This led to a significant research effort for which I required the assistance of West Point.

At the suggestion of my son, Eric USMA '98, I have changed the title to better identify the book with the sentiment expressed whenever a West Pointer is laid to rest. It is taken from the Alma Mater:

> And when our work is done,
> Our course on earth is run,
> May it be said, "Well done;
> **Be thou at peace**.

This book has no scholarly pretensions; rather it is a panorama of American military history, encouraging the reader to appreciate the enduring West Point credo of "Duty, Honor, and Country" through the lives of these West Pointers.

The two articles that I have included from Time Magazine (Jamie Malanowski) and USA Today (Rick Hampson) provide excellent "bookends" to this work with their perspective on being a West Pointer at rest in this cemetery. I am grateful for their insights.

To the families and descendents of those buried at West Point, I regret that I could not have a picture and sentence or two for all your kin. Space did not permit, but I have reserved a page near the front of the book so you may honor them with a photo or biography. I've certainly walked past each of their graves many times, often pausing to wonder about their lives and families. They all deserve mention. I hope this book will encourage others to stroll through the cemetery and reflect upon the careers and sacrifices of those warriors.

ACKNOWLEDGEMENTS

The core of this book was taken from *Home at Rest*, published in 1991, though adding a hundred individuals, their biographical information and several hundred photographs was a complex effort.   Let me acknowledge the contributions of those who made this possible.

Photographs: All photographs of the graves and the cemetery were taken by the author in several visits over three years.   The cover art was designed by the author.   Individual pictures of the West Pointers were primarily acquired through Public Affairs Office of the US Military Academy.   The overhead picture of Michie Stadium was taken from the West Point website.

Individual pictures other than the cadet yearbook photos were gleaned from the web.   In each instance, I determined that the photos were taken as part of official U.S. Army business or was published prior to 1923, thus placing them in the public domain.

Photo of the author's family was taken at an Army-Navy game in Philadelphia.   I don't recall the year or outcome, though it was quite cold.

Map: The large color map and aerial photo of the cemetery is published by the U.S. Military Academy and was taken from its website.   It is available as a handout at the Caretaker's Cottage on the grounds of the cemetery.

Text: The lengthy biographies were carried over, after editing, from the original *Home at Rest* book.   Biographies for Generals Patch, both Schwarzkopfs, Westmoreland, Harkins, Moore, and Gavin were composed by the author after reviewing their individual entries in Wikipedia.   The same is true for write-ups in the Superintendent section, Red Reader, Marty Maher, and Professor Mahan.   Write-ups in the Viet Nam, Iraq and Afghanistan sections were extracted from the individual on-line obituaries or memorial pages.   The West Point Register of Graduates published annually is a valuable resource for confirming graduation classes, service assignments/dates and date/place of death.

At West Point: Several individuals at the academy gave this book a boost along the way. Kathy Silvia USMA '80, cemetery caretaker, provided valued insights to me in the early goings of this project.

I am most grateful to Michael Brantley in the Media Relations Branch for his readiness over the past two years to scour decades of Howitzer yearbooks and scan graduation photos for me.   He also took the photograph of a recent interment for a last minute inclusion in the book - Lt. Col. Jaimie Leonard - with whom he had served in Afghanistan in 2010. Mike, you are my "Rock of the Marne".

One challenge was to locate photos of several long-deceased staff members at West Point. Their grave markers alone did not do justice. At the last minute (literally), Elaine McConnell in Special Collections delved deep for us and came up with the pictures of Old Bentz, Marty Maher, and John Saunders, some great characters in West Point lore. Imagine your photo laying around unheralded in the archives for decades and, by mere chance, someone calls it forward to present to future generations. Thank you, Elaine.

Editing and Layout: This book was written, reorganized and re-written several times over the past three years. My brother, Dr. Jeff Blomstedt, handled the layout of the text and pictures, producing numerous drafts from my re-writes. Proof reading is tedious task for which every author should be grateful to those who accept that assignment. I am, indeed, thankful for the reviews and comments by my sister-in-law, Susan LaScala, and my wife, Mae Blomstedt. It's a big "whack-a-mole" effort. Slap one down, and another appears where you have already inspected three times. Of course, if I'd stop making changes.....

Technical Advisors: I thank my son, Eric, for his contributions on the customs of West Point as well as scouting through the cemetery with me on several occasions looking for an elusive grave. More than once I received a shout from several rows over, "Dad, I just checked the web. He's buried in Arlington(or Texas or Delaware)." Tom O'Neil had indicated otherwise in *Home at Rest*, but had no photo of the grave to prove it. Sigh! Cemeteries reward the ironist.

The other day I completed a website design specification and content list for son Jeff, our technology maestro, and asked him to get it up and running ASAP. I pray it will be live before the first copies for the book are printed. Fingers crossed.....

Finally, with so many individuals, the accounts of their lives and the long history of this cemetery, certainly a few errors or significant omissions have crept into this text. For that I apologize. I welcome your suggestions & corrections by email. I will do my best fix them in a future printing.

Ed Blomstedt,
Ambler PA
August 2013
eblomstedt@blackgraygold.com

ABOUT THE AUTHOR

Ed Blomstedt was raised in Delaware and graduated from Brown University, later earning an MBA at Drexel University. He has enjoyed a management career in government and several industries. Retirement is approaching, which will allow him to complete his second book about the fictional literature of West Point.

Ed's interest in West Point began as an Assistant Scoutmaster to Troop 22, Unionville PA, when he organized weekend trips for the boys to the Hudson River Valley. On the *Volkswalk* hike starting at the Hotel Thayer, the cemetery was always a great stop for the boys and their parents to lunch and explore, although the boys seemed equally interested in the fire station across the street.

A few years later, son Eric expressed an interest in West Point, attended a summer session, and later graduated in 1998 with the top honors in economics and social sciences and an East-West Fellowship at the Univ. of Hawaii. He began his career in Armor at Camp Casey, Korea, but switched to Signals Intelligence before 9/11, later serving two tours in Iraq. Major Blomstedt is currently stationed at Ft. Meade, MD.

Ed and Mae, his wife of 40 years, have two sons and reside in Ambler PA. They regularly enjoy the Army-Navy football game in Philadelphia.

INDEX

143

CPSIA information can be obtained at www.ICGtesting.com
Printed in the USA
BVOW10*2313011013

332660BV00001B/1/P